VISITORS' HISTO

WEST SUSSEX

STONE AGE TO COLD WAR

KEVIN NEWMAN

PEN & SWORD HISTORY

First published in Great Britain in 2018 by
Pen & Sword History
An imprint of
Pen & Sword Books Ltd
Yorkshire – Philadelphia

ISBN 978 1 52670 333 0

A CIP catalogue record for this book is
available from the British Library.

Printed and bound in England
By CPI Group (UK) Ltd, Croydon, CR0 4YY
Typeset by Aura Technology and Software Services, India

Pen & Sword Books Limited incorporates the imprints of Atlas, Archaeology,
Aviation, Discovery, Family History, Fiction, History, Maritime, Military, Military
Classics, Politics, Select, Transport, True Crime, Air World, Frontline Publishing, Leo
Cooper, Remember When, Seaforth Publishing, The Praetorian Press, Wharncliffe
Local History, Wharncliffe Transport, Wharncliffe True Crime and White Owl.

For a complete list of Pen & Sword titles please contact

PEN & SWORD BOOKS LIMITED
47 Church Street, Barnsley, South Yorkshire, S70 2AS, England
E-mail: enquiries@pen-and-sword.co.uk
Website: www.pen-and-sword.co.uk

Or
PEN AND SWORD BOOKS
1950 Lawrence Rd, Havertown, PA 19083, USA
E-mail: Uspen-and-sword@casematepublishers.com
Website: www.penandswordbooks.com

To Laura with love.
Told you I'd dedicate a book to you alone eventually. X

Heading west to Washington, north of the Downs

'Sussex, when all was said and done, was not like other counties.'
Flora Poste in *Cold Comfort Farm* by Stella Gibbons

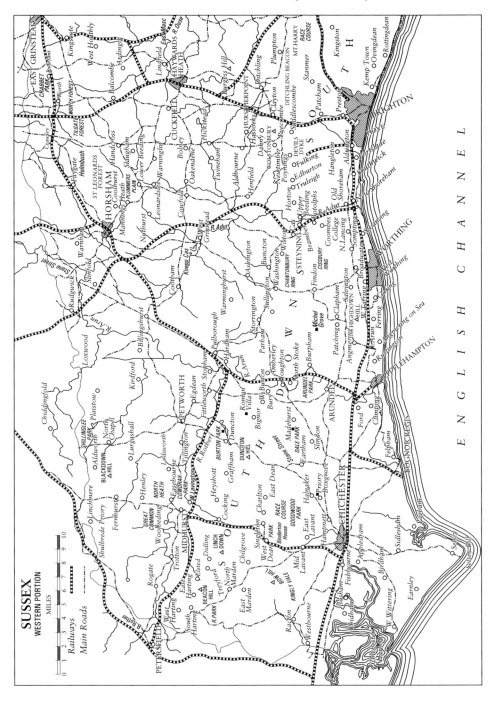

Contents

Acknowledgements

I've got a huge number of people to thank who have helped me with Visitors' Historic Sussex, *but thanks to Roni at P&S who originally commissioned the 'Visitors' Historic...' series and gave me huge help and patience when the deadline went 'whooshing by' (as Douglas Adams said). Especial thanks to Amy at P&S who has done such a staggeringly brilliant job on the book's production. Other P&S people who the book wouldn't have happened without are Felicity and Emily. Thanks to Lee and Andy for their help with the Churchill Tank on Kithurst Hill and to Antony Edmonds for the Towers postcard. Speaking of The Towers, many thanks to Sister Mary Andrew for her time and diligence in vastly improving the section on the Convent and school. My gratitude to Clare Trelfa, Headmistress at The Towers also for her support. Thank you to Richard Martin at Parham House for his unique insights into the house, its collection and inhabitants and Martin Hayes at West Sussex Library Service for his advice on the the First World War chapter. Many thanks also to Ross McLaughlin at the Dome who provided further information on the wonderful Worthing building and eternal thanks to Laura, Seth and Ed for their patience whilst I was ignoring them and writing this.*

Kevin Newman is a Brighton-born author, historian, tour guide around the city and history teacher. He has co-written history textbooks for Oxford University Press, educational film scripts and the 'Brilliant Brighton' and 'Super Sussex' supplements for the *Argus* newspaper. He has written *Brighton and Hove In 50 Buildings*, *Secret Brighton*, *50 Gems of Sussex* and *Lewes Pubs*. His next book with Pen and Sword is *Visitors' Historic Britain: East Sussex*. Following that, his subsequent work will be historical fiction about an 11-year-old boy who set up his own school in 1925. Kevin lives in West Sussex.

Introduction

Sussex is a wonderful place for visitors, whether you are visiting from elsewhere or a Sussex resident who wants to get out and about and visit lesser-known parts of their county. We start in this book with West Sussex, and the volume on East Sussex (including the separate Brighton and Hove) will follow shortly. Sussex is known primarily for the Norman Conquest and of course the misleadingly named Battle of Hastings, but there are numerous places to explore long before and in the millennium since that monumental event. Sussex is the place where the remains of the oldest human ever in Britain were discovered, and has places where dinosaurs, rhinos, bears and bison once roamed. Folk in Sussex were mining over 20ft down, a major achievement for Neolithic times nearly a millennium before Stonehenge was built. It has the site of Britain's oldest ever discovered bronze sword in Racton, which you can now see in The Novium Museum in Chichester. Sussex has a Roman king's palace, the biggest example of a non-military building outside of Italy, rare Saxon churches, military establishments founded by King Alfred, Norman castles and the only original cathedral in the country visible from the sea. Sussex boasts medieval masterpieces, stately Tudor houses, gorgeous Georgian architecture, sea bathing settlements, glorious Victorian churches and reminders of its sometimes-vital role in both the World Wars and the Cold War. It has battlefields, lost harbours, springs and river courses. On rare occasions we even have canals and castles built as hunting lodges. As Dr Samuel Johnson said to Boswell during his visit to Cowdray House before its calamitous fire, 'I should like to stay here four-and-twenty hours. We see here how our ancestors lived.' If you think you might agree with Johnson, read on and who knows—you might even end up staying longer!

The *Visitors' Historic Britain* series is an attempt to produce a literate but not overly academic guide to the different counties of the British Isles, that

Cowdray House

may or may not still be a United Kingdom by the time the series is complete! It attempts to create a modern interpretation of the guides to Sussex of the early to mid-twentieth century by writers such as E.V. Lucas and F.R. Banks who wrote Penguin's guide to the county. In this light we assume you might like to switch your GPS or satnav off and use directions from someone who knows each county well. This will take you along perhaps longer, but more scenic routes. Written directions here are under the '**Sussex without satnav**' heading.

Lucas and Banks (Penguin) were writers of their time and so the updated Lucas of 1950 or the Penguin guide were writing about the days when motoring was in its post-war infancy compared with today, and this guide reflects the needs of the twenty-first century traveller. Due to the movement needed across the county backwards and forwards and often across some distance to visit sites mentioned in chronological order, the directions are aimed at the motorist. We also mention where a site or nearby sites contain worthy visiting places of different eras, such as Bignor Roman Villa and the Neolithic Barkhale causewayed camp, up the hill from Bignor. Generally, a site is mentioned under the era it has a most interesting tale from, or when it was at its most significant, but then sometimes places with a long lifespan, such as Chichester sites can pop up several times. Generally all the sites we mention are open to the public, but where a site is currently inaccessible to the public, such as Boxgrove Man's home at Eartham Pit, we've recommended a nearby worthy place to visit. So for example here we mention an alternative that should appear in a chapter dealing with another time period: Boxgrove Priory. At time of writing, unless mentioned, all sites should be open (but not necessarily free) to the public, but if in doubt, please check with any owners or officials before venturing in! This is the first in the series, so we are finding our feet. If there are any mistakes, and I'm sure there will be, please email me on info@allinclusivehistory.org and we'll endeavour to get it right in any future reprints.

From the subject of reprints to foot and tyre prints. For the cyclist or hiker the South Downs Way is your best bet to travel between locations and certainly the most inspiring. You can also explore the route our earliest ancestors took as the first dwellers of Sussex mined, celebrated, lived and were buried along or near the Downs. This reminds us of another change since Lucas' time; much of Sussex is of course now part of the nation's 10th national park, which thankfully means the places you visit are more protected from change and development and so the growth in road traffic between Lucas' time and our own should hopefully not be replicated in the future.

This book can be read in different ways. You can either read it as a guide to Sussex and its history, or you may use it to try and explore each of the different eras of the county's past in turn. In each case, like the Romans and Saxons, we start in the West and head East, doing the opposite of one of Sussex's premier writers and poets, Belloc, who started in the east of the county in his masterpiece *The Four Men*. Of course, it is not possible to focus on every historical spot from each era, so we've tried to limit the number of sites dependent on accessibility to the public, (sometimes) how convenient the distance is from holiday destinations by car, how visually interesting the site is and how exciting historic events have been at that site. Due to the remoteness of some of the sites, it seems the best approach is unfortunately usually a mix of car and foot. Should you wish to book a tour guide to accompany you on these explorations, then we have All-Inclusive History Tours available to accompany you please call 07504 863867 or email info@allinclusivehistory.org to book or for further enquiries.

One excellent museum we haven't mentioned here, but which covers many different centuries, is the marvellous Weald and Downland Living

Museum in Singleton. It not only has rescued Sussex buildings from different ages, but has a range of activities to keep the whole family happy. It is well worth a visit.

Other Explanations

Where a site has a number next to it, it connotes a site that we have prioritized for visits—this will have directions to it and suggestions for refreshments and accommodation. We mention some sites more than once, so they only receive a number, directions, and **'Lunching locally'** suggestions with the first mention. The latter are paragraphs that provide suggestions for local pubs, restaurants, tea rooms and cafes where you can refresh yourself on your travels. All are open and correct at time of writing and we've tried to select establishments that sell or cook local Sussex produce to support local businesses. A Sussex picnic box for your travels can be ordered from The Village Larder in Washington if you want to avoid paying to eat out and can be collected from the central West Sussex spot of Washington. Call 01903 891744, email hollie@villagelarder.co.uk or go to www.villagelarder.co.uk for details of costs and availability.

This has been a very different challenge to write in comparison with my last book, which was a celebration and recommendation of my favourite parts and places of Sussex. That concerned locations I mostly knew, whereas here I was very much out of my comfort zone in places, discovering many unfamiliar sites I didn't know. This is what I love about Sussex though, and makes it a great county to get out and explore and can take you into unfamiliar territory, not far sometimes from home. Even though I have lived here most of my life and write about this county; even though my family were always taking my brother and I all over the county as young boys; even though my wife and I try and do the same with our children, there were plenty more places I found in Sussex to discover and love. I hope you will too. Many happy explorations!

Kevin Newman, Sussex 2018

Part of the path east to Storrington, north of the Downs

A Guide to Ancient Sites for Visitors in Sussex

A guide to Ancient Sites for Visitors in Sussex

'Take me to the distant past', sang the band Everything Everything and we do here indeed in this first chapter. The downside, however, of trying to understand this most 'foreign' of 'foreign countries' is that this means the chapter does need a mini-glossary. This is as we will encounter some new terminology that will be foreign to most of us. Explaining here briefly should mean we don't need to keep doing this throughout and means you can always pop back here to this guide if you forget.

Barrow Mounds and Long Barrows

We use the word 'barrow' these days usually with the prefix 'wheel' before it but the Neolithic meaning is totally different, providing us with covered burial sites, which are often found within causewayed camps. These days they will be lumps in the ground and will have been excavated long ago, so don't get your hopes up. They appear on OS Maps as the word 'tumuli' which sounds like the plural for the fawn-like creature in *The Lion, The Witch and The Wardrobe*. If you're the type of person who likes his or her prehistoric monuments to be round mounds on the numerous side, then start with Barrow Mounds. These are smaller than long barrows as they tended to have just one (presumably rich, those swines always could afford privacy) inhabitant. They're not as old as causewayed camps, as although they existed through the Iron Age and even made a flying return to fashion in the Dark Ages, they go back just a bit further to the Bronze Age, probably brought over by the nation-changing Beaker People (more about them later) around 2200 BC. The West Country is the best place for spotting these, with over 6,000 alone (must have been the lure of Bronze Age pasties, cream teas and cider), but here in Sussex we've still been generously bequested with them.

Just to make things more complicated, if you wanted earth-made ones, then you need Long Barrows, and these communal tombs could hold up to fifty adults and children and be up to 350ft long. For some reason, probably religious, ritual or to do with the rising of the sun, they tended to point easterly at their wider end, and only contained a select few members of New Stone Age Society. We have no proof of where the other 99.9 per cent of humankind ended up, and no remains to help us work this out, as it seems cremation was common. Perhaps Neolithic kebab shops stocked a different meat in those days. In all seriousness though, the flesh of those buried was removed before the bodies were buried and the bones could be used as part of ceremonies at the barrow entrances we think, so anything is possible. Despite the people who were buried in these being important, there's rarely any evidence of their life achievements. We get the odd arrowhead or smidgen of pottery, but otherwise, diddly-squat. Both types may not be that impressive now, but when built, seeing huge mounds of earth and chalk across the Sussex countryside, usually in clear spots and high up so they could have been seen from afar, would have been the Sussex equivalent of one of the Seven Wonders of the World back then.

Causewayed Camps
Dating from around 3500 BC and mostly found in the south and west of England, these are about as old as you get in terms of the English landscape. These camps used up to four sets of rings of earth banks and ditches for protection, and rather than the drawbridge of medieval castles, you had a causeway (raised walkway) to traverse to gain access to the camp, which would be protected. Despite the name, there is rarely evidence people actually camped within these, and so were the shopping centre of their day, complete with meeting place, church, area to feast. Okay, well not a shopping centre then. They can be far less exciting than a shopping centre to visit though, due to the fact most

of them have been ploughed or farmed since their inception and you sometimes have to look from above to spot that there have been banks and ditches at all.

Henges
Unlike causewayed camps, and hill forts, henges were usually constructed to be just one ring, and weren't designed to be defensive. Stonehenge would have been pretty useless for keeping out all invaders unless they were the width of Mr Creosote from *Monty Python*. They could have banks outside them, but this was presumably more for aesthetic effect and, didn't always have to have standing stones; Stonehenge's were added later and originally it was a collection of banked rings. The banks and stones vaguely served to enclose an area of land that could be as large as 12 hectares, where religious types would gather for ceremonies, dating back to about 3300 BC. Sussex is incredibly bereft of henges—it looks like we demolished one and possibly had another. Being nearer them pesky critters on the Continent, it may have been that hill forts and defensive works here were more our cup of tea here rather than religious shenanigans.

Hill Forts
Speaking of defensive works, these were needed second-most recently out of our five monuments mentioned here, only dating from the Iron Age (*c*.700 BC to 450 AD) which is practically yesterday in historic terms. As the name implies, these comprised the addition of ditches and banks, (and even stone or wood walls if you were high-tech) to hilltop sites to ensure a defensive position. Like the causewayed camps, nobody really lived there, so they weren't like Roman caestre or Saxon burhs, or even medieval castles, complete with keep, baronial hall and garrison. Their purpose was a roster point for troops or occasional protection for locals. Some were just for one family, but Sussex being relatively populous meant ours could protect whole neighbourhoods, like at Cissbury Ring. Maiden Castle is meant to be the most impressive, down in Dorset, but our very own Cissbury and Chanctonbury Ring, just for the view alone, or the size of Cissbury, take some beating.

Cissbury Hill

Ring Forts
Does what it says on the tin. Ditches and banks formed to make a ring shape. Not on a hill and generally believed to be much later than hill forts. The best sites had evidently all been developed by the Middle Ages, when most of these are built, although some archaeologists argue there is evidence they existed in the Iron Age too.

CHAPTER 1

Ancient Sussex

Visitors' Historic Sussex aims to take you to places, where, like the 'Battleground Europe' series Pen & Sword publish, events have taken place. With our first chapter on Ancient Sussex, this has, of course, not always been possible, and so the discovery of these sites may have to suffice as the event in question.

In terms of the millions of years that there has been land on this part of the earth's surface that we now call Britain today, only recently did we become an island. The few Neolithic or New Stone Age people that ended up here were initially nomadic hunter-gatherers, possibly ending up here on long-distance chases for food. The era also can be seen as when these people developed agriculture as a way of life, and stopped being nomadic hunter-gatherers. We reckon that about 4000 BC the first ideas and technology of farming, even possibly strange livestock, walked across what is now the Channel and arrived here. As a south-eastern county of England, the earliest migrants who crossed the land where the English Channel now flows would have reached this tip of the country first. Therefore it is not surprising that Sussex has some of the earliest evidence of human existence in the country.

From our earliest ancestors we have no written evidence of course. With an average lifespan of about thirty years for women and thirty-five for men, life was about surviving; scratching and hunting a living; avoiding malnutrition and suffering arthritis were priorities, not communicating. From this era there is no evidence in terms of oral traditions or nomenclature—the conquering of the county by the much later Saxons and their settlement was so thorough that the name Sussex and most Sussex place names we have had handed down to us are Saxon. There are just a few Scandinavian examples in places such as the Knabb in Brighton, Hove and the Steine in Brighton, which means 'stones' or 'stoney ground'. Celtic and Romano-Briton names such as Anderida, Noviomagus Reginorium and Atrebates became Pevensey and Chichester or were lost. Some Saxon place names such as Streat are Saxon references to a settlement built on a Roman road, but again, these are Saxon words. One of the few pre-Roman 'Celtic' names to survive is Caburn as in Mount Caburn, which originates in 'Caerbryn' (castle on the hill) and that is across the border in East Sussex, so we must leave that for the moment. Another is the Celtic 'dún', from which we get the 'Downs'. We do have the word 'coomb' or 'coombe' as in Coombes, Telscombe or Moulsecoomb, which survives here both in Sussex and in the Welsh 'cym', both referring to a valley. Lavant and Tarrant (the old name for the Adur) are both Celtic, however, the name 'Adur' (as in the West Sussex river), although tantalizingly similar to the Welsh 'dwr' for water was only a seventeenth century invention by those mistakenly believing Shoreham to be the Roman Portus Adurni. The Adur was previously also the Sore and Bramber Water before being given its current title.

For existence of human life apart from names, we can journey back in time much further. One of the earliest examples of hominids ever found in this country; the first ever 'man' to be discovered in Britain was at **1. Eartham Pit**, a quarry near **Boxgrove** east of Chichester. Dating back an unbelievable half a million years to the Middle Pleistocene Era, the man's remains were found at the pit in 1993, from excavations starting in the 1980s. This means Sussex is also the site of the largest known area of *in situ* Lower Palaeolithic land surface in the whole of Europe. We know little about this man, who seems to have reached the grand old age of his forties, as only a shin bone and two teeth have been discovered, which we assume belongs to the same individual. He could even be a she, but certainly a well-built one at an estimated height of 180cm and 14 stone. 'He' (we'll call him he for convenience) has been labelled as part of the group known as Heidelberg Man, the ancient ancestors of today's *Homo sapiens* (us in other words) and we can tell that he would have been an active individual, however, by the time his bones were gnawed at; presumably by a wolf, he was presumably not quite as active.

The tibia (shin bone) that was discovered by archaeologist Mark Roberts and his team from the Institute of Archaeology at University College London was not in any event that we can easily discern but we can infer events from his life and explain the events that have occurred at the site of his discovery. His height suggests he was from warmer grasslands on what is now mainland Europe and so the first remaining human was a migrant to what is now the British Isles, but were of course then connected to the rest of the continent by land. Perhaps this is a reminder to those wanting to sever our ties completely with our continental friends at time of writing that immigration to Britain is not a new occurrence. Flint stone tools found at the site suggest Boxgrove Man was a hunter or at least a scavenger and the hunted and cooked food he ate was cut up with some sort of device. His diet could have been interesting to say the least as the remains of bears, voles and rhinos have also been found nearby, which are of course extinct today and cannibalism on his remains could also have been a possibility. His teeth suggest toothache was a probable ailment too. Boxgrove Man was covered in a layer of gravel after his death in one of the ice ages, survived the possibility of being washed away by a stream passing nearby which has long since ceased to flow and avoided complete feasting upon by various creatures over the years. He also survived the erosion of the 200m high cliffs which he was buried at the foot of and storm debris blown up onto the beach that once existed there when this site was next to the sea. This was as a result of rising sea levels following the end of an ice age. The area has also been a marsh at one point in history, and our Heidelberg Man has survived all of this. Sussex's first proto-human lived in a very empty and lonely part of the world, and his age at death is testament to his powers of survival, let alone the half a million years his remains have survived.

Boxgrove Man has survived half a million years but you might have to wait a few more years to visit as the site which has been excavated by English Heritage, but isn't owned by them, is shockingly currently not open to the public as it is in private hands. The best suggestion as plan B is for visiting the area around Boxgrove Man's final resting place.

Boxgrove Priory is a fantastic Norman priory with much history and is open to the public for free by English Heritage. Its graveyard also has the grave of RAF pilot Billy Fiske, the first American to join the RAF, dying in 1940. Hopefully the site of Boxgrove Man, which tells so much about the very earliest humans in Sussex will be one day open to visitors.

Sussex without Satnav: You can find Boxgrove easily from the A27 east of Chichester. If you want to look in vain at Eartham Quarry, it is the next turning north off the A27 heading east from Chichester and marked 'Eartham'. From Boxgrove to our next location, you need to head west along the A27, to the first Chichester roundabout—take the last exit on your right before you would turn back onto yourself onto the A27 eastwards. This should take you to the right of a McDonalds and Pizza Hut. Follow the signs to Goodwood.

Lunch Locally: You have the George Inn close in Eartham or the Anglesey Arms pub at Halnaker.

Sussex Stayover: The Fox Goes Free pub is one mile from Goodwood at Charlton and there is also the Goodwood Hotel (once the Richmond Arms and also once next to the sea) if you wish to return this way at the end of Day 1 of any travels.

The Beedings, near Pulborough, is also another worthy site of both Pleistocene Age and Neolithic activity for devoted archaeologists. Moving forward hugely to around 5,000 years ago we head into the Neolithic, or New Stone Age. This is the time of French farmers bringing their expertise as well as their livestock and cereal crops. Sussex being so wooded and marshy at the time meant evidence from their farming were causewayed camps, long barrows and flint mines. The first were circular or oval areas, built using ditches and banks as early military establishments. Barrows seem to be areas where feasts or celebrations took place, or the marketplaces of their day. Of the four examples of causewayed camps in Sussex, two appear in West Sussex: at **2. The Trundle** and **Barkhale** near Bignor Roman Villa. Barkhale has less merit historically and less to see so perhaps it is worth visiting Barkhale when you visit Bignor. This means we have omitted it at present.

The Trundle comes from the old English word 'tryndle', meaning circle, which doesn't completely make sense, as this ancient monument (one of the oldest large ones in Britain) has straight sides in places. Its name also refers to the Iron Age hill fort, not the earlier Neolithic camp. How it was referred to seemed to change according to Saxon documents. At one point it looks as if it should have ended up being called Billingbury today. This would be an interesting contrast to the Hollingbury camp in Brighton, which we will feature in *Visitors' Historic Britain: East Sussex*. However, from far above this camp on St Roche's Hill, it does indeed look like a circle, so let's not get too picky. The hill has also become known as 'Trundle Hill' and was probably inhabited into the Roman era, although has been later used for the siting of a chapel, an eighteenth century Masonic temple and two windmills, although is home just to radio beacons today. It was the chapel of the French St Roche who gave the hill its later name, and again as with Eartham, the sea once flowed all the way to the bottom of the hill in the Palaeolithic age.

By the Neolithic era (New Stone Age 4500–2300 BC), a huge causewayed camp existed on the hill, which would be later partially built over by the Iron Age hill fort on the hilltop. In between these eras the hill became uninhabited and overgrown, and would need Iron Age warriors to clear it of overgrowth. These causewayed camps seem to be the nation's first multipurpose venues, with uses seeming to range from religious to non-religious and this one is certainly large, with only Whitehawk in Brighton competing in size. J.M. Armstrong in *A History of Sussex* event went as far as to call it 'the hilltop city of Trundle'. Excavations in 1925 revealed not only the shape of the camp, but finds included a carved Neolithic phallus. Perhaps this was waved to taunt the Belgic invaders of the Manhood Peninsula south of Chichester who were unable to conquer the Trundle and built the wonderfully named **Devil's Ditch** north of Chichester as part of their defences.

With the Neolithic dwellers of our county becoming increasingly farmers as well as livestock rearers, flints were needed to be mined to clear the dense wooded stretches of land across Sussex. Flints used as hand axes were found at the base of Trundle Hill, but for more extensive sites, **3. Harrow Hill**, north of Angmering, **4. Cissbury Down,** and **5. Church Hill in Findon** are good examples and are all found on hilltops.

Harrow Hill, like Cissbury, had flint mines dug into it in Neolithic times (4500–2300 BC) and a hilltop fort later on in the first century BC.

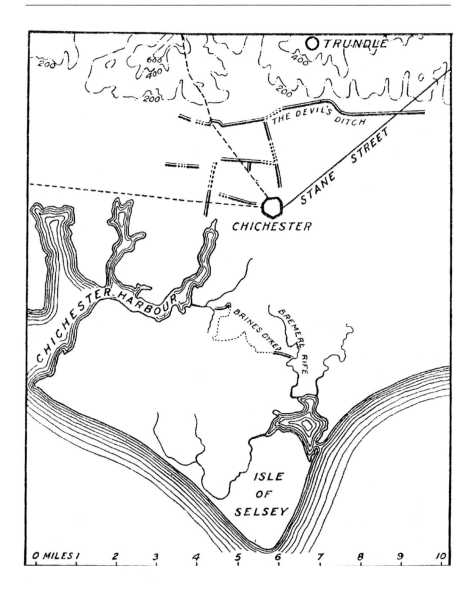

Radiocarbon dating has suggested that Harrow Hill seems to be one of the oldest flint mines, as it was dug in as early as the fourth century BC. The site seems to have been used from Neolithic times through the Bronze and Iron Ages and even up to Saxon times, so as technology improved so did the depths of mineshafts, with bronze and iron tools taking the digging down to the depth of 22ft. Like Chanctonbury Ring, worship seems to have also taken place on the hilltop as its name dates back to the Anglo-Saxon word 'hearg', which translates today into 'heathen shrine'. The name also suggests a temple graced the top of the hill at some point. Despite this, there is no evidence of burials often associated with early worship on the hill, but there is on New Barn Down, to the south-east. The people of Angmering get rather stroppy when the Harrow Hill is mistakenly described as part of much nearer Patching, which is understandable as it is somewhere to be proud of. There are only twenty examples of flint mines in the UK and understandably, Historic England declares them to be of national importance.

Sussex as a whole should also be proud that both Cissbury and Church Hill in Findon must have been one of the major industrial sites in Neolithic Britain and when combined with Sussex's other flint mines would have had a bigger output than the biggest mine in Britain, Grime's Graves. Like Harrow Hill, over 200 mineshafts have been identified. The hilltop fort that was built around the contours at Cissbury to provide the 'Ring' would not yet appear until the Iron Age. Food, rather than defence, was the order of the day in the Neolithic era. Church Hill, across what is now the A24 and on the hilltop above the western side of the valley down to Worthing was also explored in the early twentieth century. Remarkably, in one of the mineshafts the remains of a wooden ladder were found. Church Hill's mines in Findon have been carbon-dated to 4500 BC to 3750 BC, making it one of the earliest known mines in Britain. Harrow Hill in Angmering had an even more incredible find on its excavation: the archaeologists discovered soot from the miners' lamps in one of the tunnels. The people who created these flint mines are collectively known as the Windmill peasants, or Windmill people, not due to their harnessing of wind power but as one of these sites is Windmill Hill in Wiltshire. It was from the chalky hills and plains around Salisbury that migration seems to have been made eastwards along the Downs across Sussex. The Downs weren't just one of the earliest highways in the country, they were a boulevard for business in Neolithic times.

Sussex without satnav: Findon and Angmering are close together and are linked for the most part by the scenic route of the A280, known as Long

Furlong. From the Trundle, you would take the A27 but turn off onto the old A27 for Patching and Clapham to explore Harrow Hill first, which is north of the A27 and separate from Angmering village. The car parks at The Fox or World's End, further east along the old A27, may be good starting points for your walk to Harrow Hill. The World's End is closest. Alternatively, you can take a more northerly route from Boxgrove and take the A284 at Arundel and then the B2139, as Harrow Hill can be accessed from the South Downs Way and the nearest car park is Kithurst Hill, on the Downs south-east of Storrington. You can then continue on the A283 to Washington and south to Findon. This will, however, mean you miss the village of Amberley with its pretty village centre and cosy pub!

Lunch Locally: If you wish to stick to the southerly A27 route to Findon, then after Harrow Hill, for a sojourn into the pretty village of Angmering for food or accommodation, turn off the A27 at the West Worthing and Ferring/Goring junction (A2700). Avoid these two turnoffs and come back on yourself to take the final turning before going back on the A27—the Angmering Bypass which travels south-easterly. Angmering has the very cosy Lamb pub for food and drink, and more remote down a cul-de-sac towards Worthing Rugby Club is the Spotted Cow. Should you wish to continue towards the A259 you are not far from Highdown Vineyard for refreshment and purchases of the liquid kind. From Angmering back to Findon, take the Dappers Lane scenic route northerly out of the village at the fishing lake. At the top end you travel under the A27 and need to turn right onto the old A27 again, where you first reach the homely Fox, which has activities in its garden for children to explore and serves food. Continuing back along the old A27, you arrive at a roundabout that marks the start of Long Furlong, the A280 to Findon. Turn left and travel north-east along Long Furlong to Findon. Findon also has Bronze Age sites (see below) so you might want to combine exploration of these with the Neolithic flint mines mentioned above. Findon has a number of great pubs, but the best placed to explore both Cissbury and Church Hill is the Black Horse.

Sussex Stayover: Findon has no accommodation, but there is Angmering Manor or, north of Findon on the A24, there is Washington Campsite.

Washington also has several holiday cottages—Liz runs The Coach House B & B in Washington; contact liz@davidhorwood.com and the website is www.thecoachhousebnb.co.uk.

The last of the Neolithic era people to use these mines were the **Beaker People** (*c.*2900–1800 BC) who migrated to Sussex from the Low Countries and the Rhineland during the late Neolithic and early Bronze Age. They gained their name from the distinctive shape of their flat-bottomed bell-shaped drinking vessels, compared with the round-bottomed beakers of earlier Neolithic folk. Their burial and funeral traditions were also different to earlier Neolithic people. They also seemed more warlike and had more of a hierarchical society than their predecessors, the Windmill Hill people. By the 1960s, twelve Beaker Folk sites had been recorded across the whole of Sussex, but it is the Bronze Age that presents us with actual sites the visitor can explore in West Sussex; for the nearest Beaker People site of note you need to head to Lewes in East Sussex.

The Bronze Age (*c.*2300–700 BC)

The Bronze Age was colder and drier than the end of the Neolithic Age, and so the earlier safety of the peaks of the Downs became less attractive. Population growth and advances in making tools meant the wooded Weald provided better sites for homes and could be cleared more easily. This meant settlement in Sussex spread north and east of the Downs as well as south to the coast. Huge swathes of Sussex remained uninhabited, but humankind was dispersed more widely than before. Improved farming techniques meant soil at lower altitude provided greater rewards. This all means that the age has left us a greater number and types of sites to visit. There has been more evidence discovered of Bronze and later Iron Age settlement across the Weald than the much later Saxon era. Some of these Bronze Age sites we have previously mentioned due to their continued use from the Neolithic Age.

The Beaker People, mentioned above, (which is the name we usually give to the Celtic immigrants that would become Britain) experienced in the late Stone Age and early Bronze Age this new, more welcoming Briton. They seem to have taken a leadership role in the hierarchy of these times, perhaps because of their innovations with metalwork. They created metal guards for protection from firing arrows from their bows and their metalwork included copper and gold. They were later to progress, working with bronze, which the age would take its name from. Not only did they work with metal; these ancient 'Britons' would spin pots and we even think the first woven garments were from this time. All this industrious behaviour was despite them introducing the first alcoholic drink to these lands; a honey-based drink similar to mead. We as a nation owe our heavy dependency on alcohol to the Beaker People therefore, and their name is apt, they provided us not just with our first drinkers, but the drink they supped too. Perhaps the mead was much needed; there is evidence that huge volcanic eruptions in Iceland may have led to a massive drop in temperature—in just one year.

Starting with the most westerly, almost heading over into darkest Hampshire are the Devil's Humps in Stoughton, not to be confused with the Devil's Jumps in Treyford, further east. **6. Racton** is our first port of call before heading east to a Bronze Age burial ground at **7. Devil's Jumps, Treyford** and then much further east to **8. The Warrens / Sullington Warren** (burial *mounds*). We have also been left with our first evidence

The Warren

of settlements of some description as our ancestors increasingly chose farming the land rather than being nomads. This means we have Bronze Age villages or farmsteads at Black Patch, near Findon—and also at **9. Park Brow**. New Barn Down, which we have already mentioned in conjunction with Harrow Hill is another example, dating from around 1200 BC. Findon also has **10. Black Patch**, the last of our five featured flint mines after The Trundle, Harrow Hill, Church Hill and Cissbury. Our travels take us west of Worthing to **11. Highdown Hill** and we then return north over the Downs via Sompting to the Saxon town of Steyning where arrive at **12. Chanctonbury Ring** and then **13. Round Hill**, both perched above the town. Our last site from this era takes us easterly towards the border with East Sussex: **14. Wolstonbury Hill**. There are other Bronze Age sites, such as the bowl barrow at Graffham Down near Chichester, but limits of space here prevent me mentioning them all.

Racton, north of Chichester, was the site of the farmland on which a 4,000-year-old skeleton was found nearly thirty years ago, although tests to establish its age have only been implemented this decade. The tests found that, although there was uncertainty, the body was most likely to have been male and from the Early Bronze Age (*c.*2200–2100 BC), or even older and from the Chalcolithic (Copper) Age. Other human remains have been found in Sussex but Racton Man was found in a foetal or crouching position, and was reckoned to have been a priest or a king. What is even more amazing about the site at Racton, however, is not just the remains of the man that was found, but what he was holding—a bronze dagger. Although the handle, which would have been made of horn or bone and studded with twenty-eight pellets, has disappeared over the 4,000 years since the dagger owner's death, the dagger is still an exciting find as it may have been used for religious ceremonies, rituals or to sacrifice animals. The dagger is what suggests its owner was an important person as it would have been such a prized possession. Whoever its owner was, its discovery back in the 1980s means Sussex is the home of the oldest such weapons in the country.

Lunch locally: There is no pub in the tiny village of Racton but nearby Walderton has the Barley Mow, or a bit further away in Funtington is the

Fox and Hounds. The exact location of the farm where Racton Man was discovered is not in the public domain, but the skeleton is on view at The Novium Museum in Chichester, so it may be that you wish to eat in the city's many hostelries instead.

Devil's Jumps - Human bones were found by the Victorians who excavated the five Bronze Age burial mounds that are called the **Devil's Jumps**, situated on Monkton Hill, near Treyford. This cemetery is 3,000 years old and its layout corresponds with the setting sun on Midsummer's Day. The Jumps, when put together, also merit a visit as not only the longest linear barrow formation in West Sussex, but also as the best-preserved group of barrows. Like another satanic-named part of the South Downs, Devil's Dyke, it has its own myths and folklore, which, unusually it seems to have imported from another Devil's Jumps in Churt, Surrey, probably at the time in the 1700s that it picked up its name. The story goes that Thor used to perch himself on the hill at nearby Treyford and as he sat there saw the five mounds being jumped upon by the Devil who found the game amusing. Thor apparently found this less amusing and threw a stone at the Devil, which made him stop his jumping and flee. The Jumps are today protected by the Society of Sussex Downsmen, but their duties don't go so far today as to stop people copying the Devil and jumping all over them.

Sussex without Satnav: If you drive to the Hartings and turn south, you arrive at Treyford. Continue south towards the Downs as far as you can until the road peters out and park in the small chalky 'car park' (more like one parking space). Be careful though as the ruts in the chalk there mean a car can easily run aground or get its bumper stuck (Laura!!!). This involves a hefty uphill climb so Hooksway mentioned next might be easier.

Lunch locally: The Three Horseshoes in nearby Elsted means you can lunch whilst still remaining in the county and without travelling a fair distance. Your best bet though is Hooksway's Royal Oak, just off the Chichester to Petersfield road. From there you can walk to the Jumps, via a steep hill-climb.

When you are ready to flee the Devil's Jumps you have a lengthier journey east to the Bronze and Iron Age settlement at **Park Brow**, south of Chanctonbury Ring. An early settlement in such an exposed spot makes little sense today, but in the Bronze Age this part of the Downs had springs that surfaced to the water, making a village here desirable. Its nearby proximity to Cissbury Down slightly further south would also have provided industry, and movement of humans would have been nearby with a pathway passing to the west from Cissbury and any farms south of this up to the west-east trackway across the Downs at Chanctonbury, making Chanctonbury the equivalent of a busy road junction today. Park Brow was a Bronze Age commuter suburb.

The Bronze Age village at Park Brow had many features we would recognize in nearby Sussex villages in the Middle Ages. There was corn-grinding, weaving and a village pond. Sadly the first incarnation of Park Brow came to a violent end about 600 BC. This was when the first Celtic people arrived from the Continent, bringing with them the knowledge of how to make iron. They also brought violence to the villagers and apparently took over the village; burning the first Park Brow houses. Park Brow Mk II was established with the invaders' houses further up the sloping ground. We will return to the village in the Iron Age and in Roman times further on.

Site of Park Brown in the distance, to the left

Black Patch near Findon is another Bronze Age and Beaker People site that includes burial barrows, some evidence of settlement and another Neolithic flint mine. It was excavated in the 1930s by John Pull, an unusual archaeologist for the time as a working-class bank security guard when not exploring his beloved Downs. Pull was self-taught and much admired by the local villagers of Findon, eventually becoming the President of the Worthing Archaeological Society. Sadly he met a grizzly end in the Durrington branch of Lloyds where he was shot and killed in a bank raid. For a more accessible site that has also been used across several ages, we need to head the same route the bank robbers took down the A24 south to Worthing, and then turn west to Highdown Hill. This is because Black Patch Hill has no footpaths directly across it and even locals describe it as a bit disappointing and rather foreboding, living up to its dark and gloomy name. This didn't put off the Time Team crew in 2005, who also excavated the site in great secrecy. Time Team archaeologists concluded that following the end of the Neolithic flint mining phase of Black Patch's life, it became a holy place and eventually a ring barrow was built, surrounded by ritual pits.

Lunch locally: see p. 17 above for details of Findon—you also have the cafe at the Wyevale garden centre at Findon. From Park Brow, an hour's walk maximum takes to you Steyning where you have a range of cafes, pubs and restaurants, all of which are very charming. Walking west takes you to Washington.

Sussex Stayover: As mentioned, Washington has holiday accommodation and Steyning has Springwells B & B with its own swimming pool. Whilst in Steyning you can walk up Mouse Lane to the west of the town up to Chanctonbury Ring, which we feature after Highdown Hill, so it's best to cover Park Brow, Round Hill and Chanctonbury perhaps in one day. The Mouse Lane route also means you see the fantastic First World War poem 'Steyning to the Ring' (as it's become known) and you are actually taking the lane featured in that poem.

Our penultimate West Sussex Bronze Age destination involves a journey back down the Long Furlong and Titnore Lane to the A259.

Highdown Hill is a nonsensical name as 'down' is Saxon for hill anyway, so we will just call it 'Highdown'. Even so, at a miserly 226ft above sea level it is one of the more diminutive peaks of the Downs, but unusual, as a peak that ventures more southerly than other Downland peaks. This southerly viewpoint has meant it has been used from the Prehistoric age to the present day, so it is a busier visitors' spot than others we have mentioned. Highdown experienced settlement on its peak during the Bronze Age, was a fortified camp in the Iron Age, and had buildings such as a bathhouse on it in Roman times. Should the claims be true that it was the burial place of Saxon kings, even including Aelle who led Saxon domination of Sussex, then it deserves greater fame than it has as the moment. It has even been proposed that Aelle was buried here after the supposed battle with King Arthur in the late fifth or early sixth century at Mount Badon. Locally today Highdown is known as much for its ancient history, but also for being the eighteenth-century home of the 'Mad Miller', John Olliver, smuggling mastermind and the Tony Soprano or Heisenberg of his time.

Bronze Age evidence of occupation of Highdown was discovered on the south side of the hill, just inside what were the ramparts. This was led by Colonel Lane Fox during the late nineteenth century. A pit including steps, a floor, pottery and bones were found, but the prize was a bronze dagger. The find together suggested the area had experienced some sort of use for rituals, rather than being for rubbish. Later excavations uncovered long-term settlement signs such as dual-level huts, a pot, a saddle quern, hearths and a pit for cooking. Cooking was accompanied by other activities on Highdown as a loom weight and a spindle whorl were also found. It is suggested this enclosure was founded around 1000 BC in the late Bronze Age. It would not become a full fort until the Iron Age, so we shall return to it shortly.

Lunch locally / Sussex Stayover: This is easy to prescribe at Highdown— the hill has not just a (dog-friendly) tea room, complete with ice cream for dogs, but Highdown Hotel has a bar, restaurant and rooms. If this doesn't take your fancy, then the Swallows Return pub is two minutes' drive easterly towards Worthing on the A259.

It is the Bronze Age building of a hill fort which gives **Chanctonbury Ring** its Saxon name, not the crown of trees that were planted in the 1760s by local landowner Charles Goring. Its ability to provide outstanding views of any attackers and hill-upon-a-hill layout mean that it is not surprising that it had Bronze-Age remains. A burial barrow was discovered in 1958–9 and it is now strongly believed that the fort was constructed before the Iron Age, which was not always the case. Animals would have grazed within the enclosure but it would be the finding of pig heads and teeth that suggest there was a cult of worshipping pigs or the wild boar on the Ring later in Roman times. In Romano-British times later on, it certainly was a religious site as the remains of a mysterious temple with only apparently three sides have been found within the ring. It was likely that like the nearby Park Brow, there was an earlier water supply and earlier maps show signs of an 'ancient well'. It seems these may have helped the longevity of the use of the site as it seems to have continued through the Iron Age and only abandoned after about 370 AD. Chanctonbury is worth visiting as one of the most famous and visible landmarks of the South Downs, for its views, but also its historical significance across an incredible number of centuries.

Chanctonbury Ring viewed from All Saints Church, Buncton

Chanctonbury Ring

Round Hill at Steyning contains yet more Bronze Age burial mounds—at least three round barrows and a cross dyke, the latter of which is where you have a bank of earth parallel to a ditch. Flints were found in one of the barrows back in 1826, as well as apparently a skeleton which, for some reason, those unearthing it reburied the bones. The site had to wait until 1949–51 for proper archaeological work to be undertaken, supported by the nearby Steyning Grammar School. Sadly, only two years later the surface evidence of three of the barrows was obliterated by ploughing, but the earlier dig had thankfully unearthed enough evidence to establish that this was a Bronze Age burial site. Many human bones were also found as well as parts of a Bronze Age urn and later artefacts such as fourth century Roman coins and Anglo-Saxon buckles.

Considered together, these finds suggest that there was a cemetery begun in the Bronze Age and that the burial site was used repeatedly for maybe 2–3,000 years. Roman coins were either hidden or ritually placed in the grave and the buckles were Anglo-Saxon. Round barrows elsewhere were also in active use from the Bronze Age to Anglo-Saxon times. The excavations provided the answer that the site was in use for up to 5,000 years but didn't answer why burial mounds didn't seem to have been used for burying during the Bronze Age; remains were found outside the mounds in ditches but these were Anglo-Saxon in origin. In view of this another mystery was failing to be answered: Round Hill has a very prominent position on the landscape around Steyning—what exactly was its purpose and the significance of the choice of this spot in the Bronze Age? The mutilations that occurred on the Anglo-Saxon remains suggest that this was some sort of war grave, but then the further question is for what? An early battle between Saxon invaders and the Romano-Britons or a sign of a nearby Viking battle? The landscape suggests a possible military sight or watchpost; it would have been easy to defend Round Hill on three sides due to the steep Downland terrain below. The area around Round Hill hopefully has many more tales to tell.

Lunch locally: The nearest pub to Round Hill is the White Horse pub and restaurant in Steyning, which does outstanding burgers (according to my 10-year-old son!) and across from that is the award-winning Steyning Tea Rooms, which does outstanding cream teas (according to my 43-year-old wife!).

Wolstonbury Hill: Our most easterly Bronze Age site was graced with an oval-shaped late Bronze Age enclosure, similar to the enclosure on Highdown. There seem to have been flints used on the site, but no evidence of the huge mines at Cissbury and Church Hill. It was just over 1m wide and 5m deep and went across an area of just over 2 hectares. The site has been disturbed in the past by a most unusual group of archaeologists hunting for flints: the inmates of Hurstpierpoint Workhouse. Iron Age farmers didn't seem to use the site in the same way, using it instead to graze animals which may have led to further damage to the site. They also seem to have cultivated the interior of the site during the Early Iron Age. The Romans seem to have inhabited the slopes of Wolstonbury, but didn't build a temple like they did at Chanctonbury, as only the remains of pottery and coins have been discovered on the hillside. So Wolstonbury had not military purpose, but it may have inspired military action many centuries later. Winston Churchill and members of the war cabinet met at Danny House, north of the hill, and The National Trust claims that Churchill and his cabinet would allegedly visit the slopes of Wolstonbury for inspiration in the war years. Danny was also where Lloyd George and his cabinet were in the First World War when they decided to sign the Armistice. Perhaps the peaceful hills south of Danny helped bring about a willingness for peace with Germany? It's doubtful that the slopes of Wolstonbury were that quiet in the Second World War, however a few years earlier they were used by the Home Guard for target practice.

Moving from potential to actual German invaders, the Germans that settled here as Anglo-Saxons may have used the site as a cemetery, much like Highdown, according to antiquarian sources during the later Anglo-Saxon period. According to the *Gentleman's Magazine* of 1765 and 1806 the burial sites were lost due to quarrying and possibly also by the construction of the now dry dew pond. There is little to see, as much of the site that was uncovered is now back under the grass but should you venture to Wolstonbury, you can still feel smug as it is one of only two forts in South East England to have outer enclosures of the cross-bank type. This means its construction was unusual and more technical than many others. One theory that would make Wolstonbury even more special if it is ever proven, was that Wolstonbury was the home of one of Sussex's few henges (a circular or oval earthwork, surrounded by a bank and ditch, and sometimes a pattern of stones such as at Stonehenge). Wolstonbury certainly was the site of an Iron Age fort, just to the west of the hill on a visible plateau.

Our furthest easterly sites are in the Crawley area, which also has some evidence of the Bronze Age including a bronze sword, which was discovered in Langley Green in 1952. Three Bronze Age burial mounds can still be seen near the contemporaneous ridgeway track that runs between Pease Pottage and Colgate. A fourth burial mound may exist near Ifield Mill Pond.

Sussex without Satnav: From Highdown to Wolstonbury, continue east straight along the Littlehampton Road into Worthing and from there take the A27 to Brighton, A23 to Pyecombe and then walk to Wolstonbury heading north from the village. It can also be reached from Hurst (as locals call Hurstpierpoint) but the former route is recommended. If you have visited the Steyning sites last, then you can take the A283 from Steyning to Upper Beeding and then take the road south to join the A27, following the directions above or the more scenic route eastwards to Hurstpierpoint, via Small Dole, Woodmancote and keep heading east across the A23 until you reach Hurst.

Lunch Locally: For Wolstonbury, you can only reach the hill by foot or mountain bike, so it makes sense to park at the Plough at Pyecombe and lunch or have supper there. The other side of the hill provides a few pubs in Hurst. You can celebrate another Downland landmark, the Jack and Jill Windmills further east along the Downs by eating at the Jack and Jill pub below Clayton Hill. For the Crawley sites at Ifield Green there is the Royal Oak.

The Iron Age (*c.*700 BC–43 AD) - Hill Forts

The better tools that the Iron Age produced meant that settlements of bigger roundhouses were built and on Sussex hills we see the move from burial grounds to hilltop forts. The Bronze Age had seen tribal warfare as temperatures dropped and clashes over less farming land took place, but the Iron Age saw over time larger waves of Celtic immigration to the south-east. Some of which may have been peaceful migration, but the building of hill forts suggests not all were, as does the Celtic tribes soon becoming, as J.R. Armstrong says in his *A History of Sussex*, 'the dominant element'. It is incredible to consider that Sussex's Iron Age hill forts may even have been the sites of intertribal warfare—the superpowers of their day.

Moving to more peaceful matters, improving temperatures and better iron tools helped farming improve and subsequently we see more successful communities being settled in this era, in new areas too as the Weald was opened up. To get an idea of one of these communities, we need to move just outside of Sussex across the Hampshire border and visit the wonderful **Butser Ancient Farm**.

We have already mentioned the Trundle and Cissbury Ring, both of which by the third century BC were, for the time, huge hilltop cities, ringed by the necessary defensive works. Once again though we start our exploration even further west in the county at **15. Torberry Hill** in the parish of Harting. There is also an Iron Age contour fort not far away on the hill at Hammer Wood north of Iping, but Torberry is a better example as Iping is a better example of a Roman site. Torberry went through three separate development stages, starting with a rampart, with one entrance. The next stage was to develop the defences all the way around the hill, before finally extending the defences so the total area of the site went from 1 to 2.5 hectares. The size of Torberry and Cissbury suggest that in times of strife or invasion, whole communities from the wider area would shelter within these defences. The Iron Age saw a large-scale building of east-west defensive lines of earthworks north of Chichester, such as the Devil's Ditch at Ounces Barn. These were to defend Chichester and the settlement at Selsey against the hilltop city of Trundle— an interesting 'civil war' in this area at that time.

Torberry has evidence of activity on it as early as the sixth century, and it seems to have been occupied as early as the late Bronze Age. Its first defensive use was in the Early Iron Age (*c.*800–300 BC) a univallate hill fort; meaning it originally had a single circuit of ramparts for enclosure and defence. By the Middle Iron Age (300–100 BC) it was a promontory hill fort, so it included the chalk spur in the Downs here that juts out northwards to enclose the whole hilltop; forming a pear shape. In this aspect, it is almost an opposite of Highdown near Worthing, which sits on a spur of the Downs facing south towards the sea. Its resemblance to a spoon (after touching by Uri Geller!) provoked the folklore that it was created yet again by the Devil in a cross-county activity. The myth was that the Devil (who seems very busy forming parts of the Downs, it must be said!) burnt himself tasting the hot punch he was able to drink from the Devil's Punch Bowl in Surrey, and in a subsequent fit of temper, flung his spoon southwards to Sussex, where it landed and formed Torberry Hill. Quite why the name 'Devil's Spoon' therefore never caught on is a mystery, but perhaps it is because the more positive occupation by fairies is said to happen on Midsummer's Eve to chase away any evil from the Devil's cutlery! These fairies also leave us one of the nicest names of anywhere in Sussex. The indentation where a later post-medieval mill was, is today known as the 'Fairy bed'.

The fort faced major improvements and fortifications in the Iron Age, including a strengthened gateway and stone-reinforced walls replacing the earlier timber walls and earthworks. These improvements must have been substantial, as the fort still had activity inside well into the Roman era. After years as arable land and pasture for sheep, it was excavated in the 1940s and 50s but not before medieval ploughing had incurred damage. Today there is not much to see apart from a bank which was a rampart and a mostly ploughed over ditch. To see the ornaments found in the excavations, you need to travel across to Lewes Museum in the east of the county, where there are combs, knives and a spearhead. Other treasure is still said to exist however, according to Sussex folklore, that of Royalist soldiers that they buried during the Civil War. According to myth, it can only be discovered by using a golden share to plough the land. Much work will be needed to find such a ploughing tool, but this matches the work that must have been needed by our ancestors to build Torberry Hill. The walls of the ditch are thought to have been 10ft tall and by the second century BC this hilltop was an important and busy defensive site.

We return eastwards from Chichester along the A27 again to **Highdown** once more, which merits a mention in different eras as it achieved importance in both. In its incarnation as an Iron Age camp its Bronze Age features had been replaced by a hill fort composed of a single rampart and ditch. This may have been necessary due to the invasions by Belgic tribes from what is now the Continent, but it seems these changes obliterated the earlier Bronze Age settlement and its defences. Ditches were cut, which unusually for the Downs, were lined with clay, which suggests that a moat was hoped to be achieved, even if just a dry one as there is no evidence of waterworks or silt deposits. What was discovered from the Iron Age however, in one of the ditches at Highdown, was a skeleton buried under a small cairn of chalk blocks; again, unusual for this area. The fort continued to be used for burials into the Saxon era, with several more graves from then later discovered. There would be a long time between these different burials however; Highdown saw reconstruction work in the third century BC but then was abandoned until its next phase of use under the Romans.

Cissbury (further east of Highdown and just north of Worthing up the A24 at Findon) was once thought to be the main fort in the area and Highdown its southerly lookout annexe, but this was disproven when it was realized that Highdown was in fact much older as we mentioned earlier in regard to its Neolithic flint mines. The National Trust, which owns the site, has described it as 'the most historic hill on the South Downs'. It certainly has the pride of Sussex as well as being somewhere that makes Sussex proud; 'Pride of Sussex' being the name for the Round-headed Rampion flower which has been adopted as the county's official flower. Worthing is proud of its highest peak too, with the highest point of Cissbury reaching 183m (602ft) since its incorporation into the borough in 1902, especially as it is also the second biggest hill fort in the whole country, beaten by Maiden Castle in the West Country, but still one of the biggest in Europe. This pride is justified as the money to buy Cissbury was successfully raised by the people of Worthing in the 1920s, before it was happily handed over to the National Trust.

Locals may have purchased the hill, but it was incomers from another land around 250 BC who could have constructed it. Cissbury's fortifications are estimated to have been constructed either by the second of three waves of invaders from Gaul, today part of France, or to counteract their invasion. If by the Gaulicians then it was a speedy sign of their swift conquering of what is today Sussex; the fort is believed to have been built in one summer alone by thousands of slaves or local folk. If it was built this speedily by defenders, then it shows the fear and urgency this invasion from abroad provoked. The 10,000-odd whole tree trunks needed to build the wooden walls surrounding the 24-acre fort and removal of tonnes of chalk shows the importance of this area and the severity of the invasion. Cissbury faced two other invasions—one of the A27 passing or through it which has thankfully been averted; the other of preventing development of housing nearby which has not been so successful. Nevertheless, the positive invasion Cissbury faces today is that of contented walkers and ramblers, happy to climb somewhere providing views as far as Portsmouth's Spinnaker Tower and the Isle of Wight to the west and Beachy Head to the east.

16. Devil's Dyke, north of Brighton, is always worth a visit as the deepest, longest dry valley in the country; regarded by geologists as the nation's most important dry valley on chalk uplands. The adjacent hill has no name but is usually called 'the Dyke' mistakenly. It was also the home of a Victorian pleasure ground that visitors reached by its own steep railway line. It is the Iron Age fort on this unnamed hill east of Fulking Hill we focus on here. It has also been called 'Devil's Dyke Camp'; taking its name from the coombe or valley next to it but had the more romantic name of 'Poor Man's Walls' in the late 1700s according to a map. Communities had grown up around the valley and its adjacent hilltop peak of the Downs during the Bronze Age but the necessities of the Iron Age led to this further defence being constructed. Its remains are less impressive than Cissbury, but we still have some ramparts on view and round barrows. Excavations suggest it started in the early age as a small enclosure but the whole later site wasn't in full use until the late Iron Age (100 BC–43 AD).

Devil's Dyke is less satisfactory as an ancient history site as it is far smaller than other forts and harder to imagine at its peak. Less is known about the fort than others. It appears the fort started on the highest peak of the hill as a small enclosure and then extended to the north-east side of the hill. Excavations have shone less light on the site than others—a single skeleton was the prime find apart from flints suggesting it could have Neolithic origins as a settlement or mine, whereas other finds suggest later Bronze Age activity. The nice thing about the hill fort at Devil's Dyke though, is it appears that you drive into it; the current road marks the approach to what archaeologists think was the entrance. Near to this entrance on the south-west are the most visible remains, an outer ditch and bank made of ramparts. There are less signs of this on the steeper northern side, which had less need for them due to their near-vertical drop, but there is evidence of one bank and ditch, which appears as a dark green strip of grass. The hill fort may not have had a name since the 1700s and the hill on which it sits may not have a name, but the 360° views from its 711 ft peak are some of the most breathtaking on the Downs and unmissable. What it lacks in size, scale and historical remains, the fort at Devil's Dyke Hill makes up for with its panoramic vistas.

Sussex without Satnav: For drivers from Cissbury you travel south down the A24 and then east along the A27 until the Hove/Devil's Dyke turnoff. At the roundabout you reach, take the first left and then branch off left as the road forks to the right along the top of Waterhall Valley to Saddlescombe. This is one of the most scenic car journeys Brighton has to offer along its 'rooftops' of the Downs. The Dyke can also be reached from the north of the Downs and offers an equally scenic and more rural ride. Traffic and parking can be a problem in the Dyke's car parks on sunny days and so the Brighton and Hove open-top bus from numerous stops in Brighton is recommended and makes the visit for Brighton-based visitors even more special.

Lunch locally: The Devil's Dyke pub on top of the hill has a convenient bar and restaurant but it can be heaving on bank holidays and other busy times, so a recommended walk down the hill to Fulking would be recommended to the much more historic Shepherd and Dog pub, which has its own Downland spring as well as a large beer garden. The Royal Oak at Poynings below the Dyke is also within walking distance and is a smashing family-run pub.

17. Ditchling Beacon again like Devil's Dyke presents some of the most breathtaking views from the top of the Downs. Due to its lack of a large car park or hilltop inn it suffers fewer crowds than its more westerly rival. It is no less spectacular though, and its Iron Age camp is one of the larger defences from this period. It is definitely earlier in its construction than the Dyke's camp but, like that, has produced few interesting finds from this era. Yet again ploughing has done much damage, but bone and antlers have still been found. Its name comes from the Saxon-named village to the north below, with the 'beacon' aspect referring to beacons lit at its summit from times that needed warnings of coastal attacks, the medieval and early modern eras. The most famous of these was the Armada of 1588 of course, but it shows we have again an Iron Age construction with a much later name. Early maps have the site named as 'Ditchling Castle', which although inaccurate suggest the site has had a range of names. Like Devil's Dyke, Ditchling Beacon could even predate the Iron Age as flint usage has again been shown as occurring on the hill and avoids artificial defences to the north, relying instead on the steep northerly slopes here also.

Sussex without Satnav: Ditchling Beacon is further east along the A27 from Devil's Dyke—this time a picturesque hilltop drive along Ditchling Road is necessary. For walkers, the walk from Dyke to Beacon is energizing and a windy wonderland of constantly inspiring views.

Lunch Locally: It is possible to travel from the Dyke to the Beacon using the roads north of the Downs, however, it involves turning back on yourself slightly using the A23 by Clayton, but this is another worthwhile and very pretty drive. It also presents the best lunching opportunities at Tortington Manor, the Shepherd and Dog in Fulking and Royal Oak in Poynings, both previously mentioned. The Ginger Fox at Shaves Wood and Rushfield Garden Centre just north of the Dyke and Saddlescombe provide good lunch options too, with Rushfields having a farm shop as well as a wonderful cafe. You still have the (previously mentioned) Jack and Jill pub in Clayton and numerous dining opportunities with the pubs in Ditchling. All in all, a range of choices to prepare you should you wish to climb the Beacon from sea level north of the Downs.

Iron Age Villages

The Iron Age was a time of increasing settlement as well as the building of hilltop defences and Sussex had over thirty hamlets north of Brighton alone between the Adur and the Ouse. Here though we focus on just one as we return now once more to **Park Brow**, which you will remember is north of Cissbury Ring and just south of Chanctonbury Ring.

Park Brow 'Mk II' was a very different settlement from its nearby Bronze Age forerunner. Although the building materials were still wattle and daub, the houses from this era were much bigger and this time the settlement was defended by a timber trench and ditch. The remains of one house showed it to be comparable in size to our houses today – 15m long by 60m wide and big enough for fifty people. Iron Age Park Brow residents seemed to have had a more luxurious life than their forebears; with higher-quality pottery, as well as the same corn-grinding, use of storage and weaving of the first 'Park Browers'. If you visit Park Brow today you can still see an ancient trackway that these residents would have used and it makes sense to try and fit in Cissbury and also Chanctonbury if you can, as it is likely that 'Park Browers' would have interacted with at least one of these.

It seems life became increasingly hard for the residents of this Iron Age village though. A pit, which was previously believed to be a meeting place for villagers, seems now to have been an attempt at rain collecting; perhaps as the Downland springs that supplied the village dried up. Whatever the reason, around the time by the start of the third century BC and the end of the fourth the village had moved yet again, this time to a more southerly location once more and Park Brow Mk II seems to have prospered until further changes under Roman invasion and occupation. We will encounter Park Brow again in its last and final phase under the Romans.

Iron Age Places of Worship

18. Lancing Ring, up on Lancing Down north of North Lancing, is a small late Iron Age shrine, within a banjo enclosure, so named because of its shape, which is unique in Sussex. The name seems confusing when compared with Cissbury and Chanctonbury, which have rings dating back from their use as military sites. Lancing is worth a visit though for the fact it is a rare and diverse habitat that has the unusual plant called broomrape growing there; a member of the pea family. Early Purple Orchids can be seen in the woodland in the springtime and the dew pond is home to numerous newts, adders and sometimes lizards can sometimes be spotted in sunlit areas. The wildlife may be wonderful, but so could be the age of the site if the friends of Lancing Ring are correct. They claim that the track alongside Lancing Ring may be of Neolithic origin (*c.*4000–2000 BC). It is certainly true that the area has evidence that goes back far earlier: the earliest known mention of archaeological remains in the area is an Acheulian hand axe, perhaps dating to 200,000–100,000 BC found west of the Ring and to the east of Lancing College Chapel. The Iron Age shrine at Lancing Ring was discovered in 1828 and like Chanctonbury it appears that it was also a temple in Roman times. This leads us onto our next chapter and our next era, with the Roman invasion and occupation dating from the first century BC.

Sussex Without Satnav: From Park Brow, walk back to the car park at Findon and drive south to Worthing's Offington roundabout where you join the A27. Travel east on the A27 to Lancing and at Lancing Manor roundabout just before Shoreham Airport, turn left into North Lancing, the oldest and most interesting part of the 'village' as Lancing still incredulously declare themselves to be. Head as far north as you can uphill, and Lancing Ring is a short walk from the very top roads in North Lancing.

Lunch Locally: Miller and Carter have one of their steakhouses in North Lancing; other than that, the area is pretty thin on the ground for eateries.

CHAPTER 2

Roman Sussex

The Belgic Atrebates tribe who settled across Sussex and East Hampshire were an advance boarding party for the Romans in 75 BC. The Atrebates, very aptly as their name means 'settlers', settled in what is today the area around Chichester. They developed the area south-west of Selsey as one of their administrative centres, their main base being Silchester in Hampshire. This area has now been partly submerged under the waves as Selsey ceased to be an island and the coastline changed, so we are not able to visit the site as we suspect it is without scuba gear. The Atrebates, who were linked to a fellow Atrebates tribe in Northern France, give their name to the city of Arras today, and to the area of Artois. They may have settled around Chichester, but it would not be until 42 AD that the Roman invasion proper invaded these parts, led by the wonderfully named Titus Flavius Vespasianus who would later become the Emperor Vespasian. The Roman policy was co-operation as well as conflict where needed, so they had dealings with the local King Cogidubnus, who ruled as king in the Chichester area, so this is back where we start again. The Romans are believed to have allowed the building of our first site we can visit from the Romans, **1. Fishbourne Roman Palace**, possibly as a thank-you present to Cogidubnus for his co-operation. They also gave him the less-than snappy title *Rex et legatus Augusti in Britannia* (King and Legate for Emperor Augustus in Britain). Who wouldn't want that? The principality of Cogidubnus died with him and his territory became submerged as part of the Roman province. Likewise, the southern end of Fishbourne's palace is today partially submerged under the road and village of Fishbourne, but when complete would have been larger than Buckingham Palace today. It would have also overlooked the Roman bridgehead that was Fishbourne.

Fishbourne Roman Palace is not just one of Sussex's oldest buildings, but the largest civilian Roman building north of the Alps. It is incredible that to find a better Roman dwelling we need nearly to go to Rome, so blessed is Sussex with these remains of international architectural and historic importance. What is even more remarkable is that this huge Roman palace was only properly discovered as recently as 1960. It has the earliest garden in Britain too, as well as the largest collection of mosaics *in situ* in the UK. Fishbourne's ability to inspire awe and wonder doesn't stop there either, as behind the scenes in the Collections Discovery Centre are over half a million artefacts, many of which have never been seen by the public. Although much is under the buildings of Fishbourne, we can tell that there was at least a great central court and three secondary small courtyards within the myriad of rooms in this complex. Its early construction date suggests it was built to oversee the invasion develop and impress soldiers and officials arriving from the rest of the empire. Its size and large symmetrical layout suggests that although it could have been Cogidubnus' home, it was also an administrative centre. The palace's two centuries from 75 AD until its destruction by fire around 270 AD saw much happening, and this is reflected still today in the wide range of events the palace offers to visitors, academics and schools. This is as you'd expect from Sussex Past, the trust that also runs Lewes Castle and Anne of Cleves House, and who always ensure visitors can do and touch as well as see and hear in their properties. Visitors are offered not just guided tours but an introductory film, the chance to see curators at work, re-enactments and the chance for young ones to try their hands at archaeology.

The setting at **Fishbourne** is nearly as wonderful as the palace too. Walking around the historic village of Fishbourne, you can imagine how the harbour was once a thriving place of commerce and the gateway for the Romans to this part of the world. It was this harbour that made the construction of Roman Chichester, or Noviomagus Reginorum as it was called, a necessity. A trip to the palace and its surrounding village are well worth braving the seemingly endless roundabouts of the A27 around Chichester for. Alternatively, the train journey is easier and ensures you enjoy the wonderful view of this ancient part of Sussex. The view of the palace sadly could have been even greater—it was undergoing further redevelopments when it met its end by fire. We can only imagine how magnificent a Roman palace here in Sussex that had survived the third

Dell Quay

century might be still today. If it was built for Cogidubnus, then this means that when you walk around Fishbourne, you walk around the domain of what was possibly the home of an early British king. Not many places in the country can claim that!

Fishbourne, or perhaps Copperas Gap to the south of it, near **Dell Quay** today was possibly where the Roman mega-motorway, Stane Street, terminated into Chichester harbour. One of the most picturesque parts of Chichester harbour is **Bosham**, which is a village with a quayside today that was first inhabited by the Romans and though they may not have built much in the way of aqueducts in Britain, they did create the Millstream which exists still today, still bringing fresh water through the village that was lacking on their arrival. Pevsner talks of the Roman Basilica that was said to be on the site where the church now is. Bosham may have been inhabited by the Romans but it came into its own more in the Anglo-Saxon age, however, and so we will return to it later.

Bosham

Heading to the north-east of Bosham, **2. Chichester**, or Noviomagus Regnenses as it was known, the 'New Market' as it translated, became a large Roman settlement for two reasons: it skirted Stane Street to the south and was the first marketplace to be built with East-West routes linked to and from it—part of the existing route from Havant to Portslade. The East-West Sussex highway, the Greensand Way was to leave Stane Street and head east from Hardham instead, travelling to Barcombe Mills in East Sussex. Here it joined a north-south route to Lewes which seems to have been for the transport of resources also to the new Roman city of Londinium as it would become.

A mass of further archaeological finds awaits us under Chichester, but we are lucky that the latest, the footings of two town houses, have found been under **Priory Park** and so this has never been built over. You may think that finding Roman houses in a Roman town is not especially remarkable, but due to the fact Priory Park was preserved for a monastery the land has never been built on since Roman times so these remains were well preserved. Chichester having no sewers until the 1880s meant much in the way of archaeological finds have disappeared as residents had to dig holes to deposit their bodily waste for over a thousand years. Sadly, a whole street in Priory Park must have been destroyed when a reservoir was constructed there as recently as the Second World War.

On the positive side, Priory Park's houses are amazing as they were discovered using radar; something our Victorian archaeologist ancestors could only have dreamt of! Furthermore, the remains of these large buildings (bigger than Pallant House Gallery) are in an incredibly complete state. We can tell the houses have walls surrounding complete rooms, based around a courtyard or atrium and were in an unusual oblong shape. This discovery in Priory Park is one of the most important of recent years and the fact it showed one of the houses had a bathhouse and hot room means we now know Chichester had at least two bathhouses; suggesting that cleanliness was even more prevalent in the city that we thought. It also means water must have been supplied to the area where the park is. The bathhouse would probably have been a more private bathhouse as the houses were luxurious ones with Chichester Council's archaeologist, James Kenny, estimating that their modern equivalents would be worth millions today. These houses were built from the best materials by architectural experts of the day with underfloor heating and would have needed a street connecting them to the rest of the city. This street has been revealed by radar scans leading east out of the park, however, the Council has decided to leave that under wraps for the moment. These rich Romans have left us with a mystery, however. One of the buildings; a deep masonry building with a rounded end has left archaeologists scratching their heads as to its purpose. The remains of a second Roman road were also discovered but no decision has been made since to dig to explore this. Chichester evidently has more secrets still to unveil and the city plans lottery funding at time of writing to show this exciting find to the world once the site is returned to normal and Priory Park to its usual oasis of green tranquillity within a busy city. Priory Park is one of the nicest parts of the city today; evidently rich Romans thought the same too.

For the masses rather than the few, a Roman **3. Amphitheatre** existed just to the east of the town outside the East Gate in the small park by Whyke Lane. This is as the amphitheatre was outside of the city limits and the later walls. The building of the walls seems to have corresponded with the end of its lifespan as archaeological excavations show its time of use was between the first and third centuries. Business and pleasure for up to 800 spectators were both on the menu here at the 200ft long amphitheatre, as it was used for games and combat but also, it is believed, business transactions. Perhaps the concept of the TV show *The Apprentice* is not that new. Gladiators fighting until one met a grizzly end did occur here, but mainly it was sports of the animal kind with bear-baiting and cockfighting, sports that continued across the country into the nineteenth century.

For something truly visible, another second century AD bathhouse is now the home to the **4. Novium Museum** just north of the cathedral and the cathedral itself has Roman remains underneath it you can view through a glass floor panel. The Novium will have the finds from the recent Priory Park dig on display in future.

It seems logical that a 'new market' town must have been needed so near to what is now Chichester Harbour before the Romans came, and historians believe that the Romans simply shored up the defences of this settlement. Although the garrison's walls didn't come until later during the 367-year occupation of Sussex, the Romans needed to defend this territory and the approach to their supply route into Britain as other harbours on the Sussex coast didn't seem a Roman priority. We only have a limited idea of the Roman layout of Chichester but know that the area north of where the market cross is today seems to be the epicentre and the site of the market cross the crossroads of the joining of the road north-south and east-west. West Street had a set of baths in their vicinity, but much else is a mystery inside where the city's walls were later built. It is a good thing therefore that we have the road layout of the city, which is much the same as the Roman layout. We also thankfully have a fantastic relic of Roman Chichester in the Minerva stone in North Street and a large amount of the city's walls remaining.

The Minerva stone was found in 1723 and today can be seen resited in the wall of the Assembly Hall and tells of the city's maritime links, reminding us that the remains of a temple lurk somewhere under the city. It translates as saying 'To Neptune and Minerva this temple is dedicated for the welfare of the divine House by the authority of Claudius Cogidubnus, King and Legate of Augustus in Britain by members of the guild of Craftsmen'. For Chichester's walls, we have the Victorians to thank as they were passionate about walking around and along them. The walls are mostly medieval rather than Roman but are built on Roman foundations and we still have one of the sixteen identified bastions; the defensive towers that were added to the walls after 275 AD. This was as their purpose changed from financial

A rebuilt section of the walls

and for demonstrating status to defensive. Chichester's walls, constructed in the third century are amazingly 80 per cent still identifiable and the best example of a walled town in the south of England. Even better, the whole nearly mile-and-a-half circuit is mostly still accessible, and actually walkable upon. The exterior complete with bastion is best viewed from Westgate Fields.

Leaving the walls behind, we travel up Stane Street and journey past Bignor Roman Villa. Soon after the initial invasion, the occupying Roman families of leading soldiers and administrators would need villas for their large families and servants.

5. Bignor is a great example of a villa site and has mosaics as good as anywhere in Britain today from our Roman forebears. Like Fishbourne Roman Palace it was discovered by accident, but over a century earlier in 1811, meaning it helped greatly to provoke the Victorians' interest in the Romans. Although smaller than Fishbourne, with sixty-five rooms at its peak it is still one of the biggest and best known Roman Villas remaining in the country, with a more agricultural purpose than Fishbourne. It may have been the equivalent of a manor house owned by a rich Roman farmer rather than a palace, but it was instrumental in helping nineteenth century academics learn more about how wealthy Romans lived. It also has the country's longest Roman corridor on display. Not many historic attractions in Britain have been owned by one family and open for over 200 years, one of our biggest Roman villas and the country's most famous Roman sites. It seems Bignor met a less violent end than Fishbourne, possibly as it was safer from raiding attackers than its seashore sibling at Fishbourne. Fishbourne was destroyed in flames, Bignor died by neglect, slowly being forgotten about. With such amazing mosaics and reminders of our Roman past, it's certainly unlikely to be forgotten about again.

Note: As a family-owned attraction (actually the same family who discovered it) Bignor only opens from spring to Autumn. Bignor opens in March every year. If I owned a Roman Villa (or at least its remains), I'd want it all to myself too for half the year. Just in case you skipped Chapter 1 (don't blame you!), you might want to visit Barkhale causewayed camp, up the hill to Bignor.

Sussex without Satnav: From the Chichester Ring Road, the prettiest route is the northerly route by taking the A285 to Bignor. Slightly faster, but also scenic is the A27 to Fontwell and then the A29 to Bury where you head west to Bignor. The Roman Villa is well signposted from both.

Lunch Locally: Bignor is the perfect opportunity to visit the award-winning Nyetimber vineyard. There's no pub in Bignor but nearby Sutton has the White Horse Inn if you don't want a solely liquid lunch at Nyetimber. Between 50–100 AD building of villas commenced at Sidlesham, Hardham, Arundel and Angmering, but we return next to **6. Highdown** again, outside of Worthing for a villa with another bathhouse.

Highdown - The exciting thing about Roman Highdown is that we know there was a villa there, but it hasn't yet been found. The bathhouse, on the west side of the hill halfway down the slope, is probably linked to the villa, as the villa nearby at Angmering seems a little distant for Romans, some of whom would have been used to the warmth of the Mediterranean to be wandering in a towel. It's thought the cusp of the first or second centuries is the most likely date for the bathhouse's construction and it was built on a site that had been used during the later section of the Iron Age; for what we know not.

We would have had the remains of a third Roman villa in West Sussex to take you to had not developers built over the villa at Southwick, half in the 1930s and the rest in the 1960s with a road, Manor Hall Road, cutting right through it and houses later on. Manor Hall Road in Southwick is where a first century AD Roman villa, elaborately and lavishly decorated existed, but the site was sold to property developers who built homes and the Methodist Church on the site. At least the site is remembered today with road names such as Roman Road and Roman Crescent. There is an information board today at the site and the location is scheduled as an ancient monument by Historic England.

Sussex without Satnav: From Bignor, take West Burton Lane back to Bury Hill and then head south back down the A29 and A284 to the A27 and then at the West Worthing turnoff, back down the A280 again to Angmering and east along the A259.

At the risk of following the exploits of the historical version of *EastEnders*, we're once more back into Worthing and up the A24 to visit the good folk of Park Brow again. The Romans' expertise at building was clearly felt at Park Brow as houses were still of a decent size (25 by 30ft) but now boasted plastering and were painted red, cream and grey. Iron nails now attached red tiles to the roofs, doors had keys and glass windows existed; there is also the possibility floors were even laid with wooden floorboards. Diets were more lavish thanks to Roman imports of fruit and vegetables which were starting to accompany the traditional Briton's diet of bread, meat, meat, bread and some more meat. We can tell this from the village's Roman rubbish pits, which also show life was more varied too by Roman times, with decorated pottery, brooches, bracelets and rings. Villagers had a choice of pottery and owned both locally-made as well as imported pottery.

This was the best time to live in Park Brow throughout all its incarnations, and it was also the last time the windy hilltop Downland site would be used. Saxon houses would be built lower down in cleared woods of the Weald and chalkland plains south of the Downs, more similar to the lowland settlements the next set of invaders from North Germany and

Jutland were used to. Houses would be homely but never experience the level of building expertise Roman ones had. Saying all this, you'd expect Park Brow's Roman remains to be substantial still today. The houses still contained much wood though of course, and the walls underneath the plaster were still wattle and daub so the village was still susceptible to fire. This was what it experienced soon after 270 AD, the same time Chichester's walls were being reinforced with defensive bastions against attacks and a villa at the site of Springfield Road in Brighton today was burnt down. Park Brow was not alone; Fishbourne Roman Palace was consumed by flames around this time. Attacks by coastal raiders from Germany, the one group of people the Romans couldn't conquer, were now evidently having an impact across Sussex.

Saxons disliked living on the hills and in Roman buildings; they often believed them haunted. The Park Brow building materials that remained would have been sought after by the invaders who settled lower down on plainland or in the valleys Saxons favoured. Ploughing throughout the twentieth century obliterated much of the remains of the signs of the earliest past of Park Brow. So today, apart from the evidence of early lynchets (banks of earth that collected over time due to ploughing) when the sunlight is angled at certain times of the year, there is sadly little to see of this unique Sussex settlement that survived from humankind's earliest days in this county up to the time of its mightiest invaders. Today, to see the nearest settlement that perhaps we have to Park Brow, you need to travel to East Sussex to Telscombe to see a settlement perched high on top of the Downs. Even Telscombe though is not quite on top of the Downs as Park Brow was not as exposed to the elements. These hardy ancestors of ours really were living on top of their world.

Whilst at Park Brow, it makes sense to walk the short hop north to Chanctonbury Ring where the Roman temples once were. This site is easy to find as although there is no visible evidence, it is within the earthworks that formed the Iron Age hill fort and the later circular ring of trees that were replanted on top of the ring in 1990 following the 1987 hurricane. It seems the Roman temples followed some sort of Iron Age religious activity and remains of parts of pig's bodies suggests the possibility of worship of pigs or wild boars, which ties in with similar findings on other

Chanctonbury Ring

local sites. Chanctonbury is a mysterious place, and so it is suitably fitting that the remains of both temples are unable to tell us if they both existed at the same time and even why both of the temples seem to have no east side or entrance apparently. They were definitely grand and sturdy affairs though—the more northerly temple had 2 and 3ft thick walls, plastered and built with flint and mortar. It was square in shape, whereas the more southerly one was octagonal. Finds of tessellated tiles suggest the floors of these lofty places of worship were covered in mosaics—it would have been interesting to find out if wild boar were commemorated here too.

Walkable from Chanctonbury is **7. Lancing Ring**, which we mentioned earlier on. The temple, which is 200yds west of the Ring was discovered in 1828 and like Chanctonbury, seems to have had an Iron Age religious purpose too. There seems to be a range of Iron Age forts where Romano-British temples and shrines were constructed inside them, so perhaps as with today they had tendencies for worship to take place in historic sites. Lancing's Roman temple was probably constructed in the first half of the Roman era and its walls, like Chanctonbury's, were built with flint and plastered, but this time painted red. It was a hefty building too, with a 40ft^2 total surface area and a central building that was 22ft^2. Like Chanctonbury it faced east. This may have been to escape our prevailing south-westerly wind or perhaps our ancestors here and at Chanctonbury practised their worship as the sun rose in the east?

With the increasing attacks on Britain from abroad by the fourth century AD and troubles in the Roman heartland forcing the Roman army home, by 410 AD the sun was no longer rising, but instead setting on the Roman adventure in Britain. It would be the Saxons that would be the new dominant force in Sussex and it is now to these raiders, invaders and eventually settlers we turn our attention.

CHAPTER 3

Saxon and Viking Sussex

There is something very special about being entrusted to write about Saxon Sussex. It is hard not to feel honoured when asked to describe the events, buildings and achievements of the people who gave Sussex most of its place names, and even the name Sussex. We must remember these people; after all, our county is not the name of a place; it is named after *people*. We live in [the kingdom of the] SudSeaxe, the South Saxons; these people cut off from the more northerly Saxon tribes on the South Ridge of the Thames (Surrey), separated from the East Saxons by the Weald, Kent and London and apart from the West Saxons who would eventually take over the territory of the South Saxons to form one kingdom. Sussex was not all about just the South Saxons, however, the Haestingas were very much a separate people, probably from Jutland rather than Germany but even they too were subsumed into the South Saxon territory by the Middle Ages.

We now have much more in the way of events to explore as we move away from the Roman era. In West Sussex anyway, there was the invasion through Chichester Harbour, the building of roads and presumably battles, but the subduing of Sussex involved more in the way of construction and co-operation than any huge battles we know of. Saxon empire-building was different; we have a mass of burial sites and battlefields as they conquered their way across the county and then further battles as the Vikings, centuries later, tried to repeat the achievement. We forget that the Saxons were just as brutal and bloodthirsty as their Viking successors, which, coupled with the far greater building and naming the Saxons achieved that survives, gives us more to see, visit and tell about than from Roman Sussex. Dr Geoffrey Mead, local historian, calls them 'The great ethnic cleansers' and this is true; the Saxons eradicated most evidence of previous inhabitants' place names.

The biggest and most dramatic clash we can put a location to, between Roman-Britons and the new wave of invaders, the Saxons happened at the eastern end of the county. A mass killing of Britons within the Roman walls at Anderitum (Pevensey) took place but being in East Sussex we must leave that for the sequel to this book. The landing of the Saxons in 477 AD is believed to have been achieved at Selsey, and a possible second landing at Shoreham though so we don't miss out on all the action. The landing bridgehead became christened Cymensora, which has been claimed to be a range of places, the most logical of which in terms of similarity of names would be Shoreham. Most historians believe today though that the landing place, from which the chief invader's son Cymen apparently gave his name is now under the waves at Selsey. Its name suggests either Cymen was first ashore before his father, the future king of Sussex, Aelle or he led the first battle against the Britons. Cymen is mentioned first in the *Anglo-Saxon Chronicle* which is all we have to base our knowledge on, suggesting he was perhaps the oldest, where it says that Aella and his three sons 'slew many Welsh, and some they drove in flight into the wood that is named Andreds-lea'. Cymensora seems to be indicated by the Owers bank on nautical charts; a little offshore of Selsey.

Soon the Saxon Shore (as the Romans called the coast where they had to defend against the Saxons) would become the Saxons' shore as Aelle and his sons moved ever eastward. The very different coastline in the fifth century AD would have seemed familiar to the Saxons to their homelands of North Germany and South Denmark (there was no one 'Saxon' tribe, but actually a mix of races that invaded). During this westwards progress across Sussex a battle took place being of sufficient significance to have been passed down the centuries to its recording at the time of the *Anglo-Saxon Chronicle*. This was on the banks of the Mercredesburn, a river we presume is in Sussex as it was in 485 AD and the Saxons made it further east to Pevensey by 491 AD where they slew the Saxons within its walls after a final siege. This saga will no doubt be a series of Bernard Cornwell novels in time, but Mercredesburn will need Cornwell's usual conjecture to locate, although some have claimed it is Seaford as 'Mer' and 'cred' meaning 'sea' and 'ford' but in a mix of Celtic and Saxon language—the Ouse and Cuckmere rivers are both hot favourites as the Mercredes.

Alec Barr-Hamilton in *In Saxon Sussex* suggests another site, that of Slonk Hill, north of Shoreham, based on oral traditions of a battle there and the writings of Cheal, the Shoreham historian who suggests 'slonk' as the ancient word for slaughter. His other argument is that it is a neat halfway stage between the conquering of Selsey in 477 and Pevensey in 491. This seems too neat; supposing Cymensora, Chichester and Lancing are named after where Aelle's sons *fell* in battle then progress easterly was a lot slower than this. Slonk Hill did, however, have a stream called the Northbourne at that point which flowed down into the Adur at that spot.

My personal view is that likely possibilities were Burpham or Bury on the Adur—a 'sea ford' creates the possibility of tidal rivers, and the later Saxons built on existing sites to create their burhs. Conquerors traditionally fortify the sites they struggled to capture so that further conquerors attempting to repeat their achievements struggle. It seems either the Arun or the Adur was another subdivision of Saxon Sussex, so the crossing of it has some significance to the Saxons, which could have come about due to a battle. Timothy Venning in *The Kings & Queens of Anglo-Saxon England* translates 'Mearcreadesburn' as 'border stream', which gives further credence to the Arun or Adur being the Mercredesburn. A cross-Sussex route to Pevensey along Downland makes more sense than keeping an army advancing solely along the coast, where it could be more easily surrounded. J.R. Armstrong in *A History of Sussex* suggests the Battle of Mercredesburn was in the west of Sussex, and that it was probably 'near the border with Hampshire'. This is possible in view of the name of the river, but it seems unlikely that the small journey to the border with Hampshire from nearby Selsey took at least eight years from 477–485, when the campaign eastwards across most of the county, following the sites of over a dozen burial places, would take only six years to get to Pevensey in 491 AD. This all assumes the dates given to us in the *Anglo-Saxon Chronicle* centuries later were correct, or that these battles happened at all! The *Chronicle* was working from oral traditions passed down over the centuries so could be widely inaccurate, or Alfred's scribes writing the *Chronicle* may have created past mythical battles to inspire his generation of Saxons, battling another nation once more; this time for their homeland.

East Sussex has its own claims for being the site for the battle. Some historians believe a treaty signed in the Ouse Valley suggests a consequence of the battle site. The site of Town Creep near Ashburnham—it has the possibility that the 'creep' part of the name is 'Mecredes' changed over time and oral tradition in the area was that a town on the site was destroyed by the Saxons. It even has a small river, with a 'bourne' in its title, the Ashbourne running nearby. Perhaps the river in question was a tributary or much larger in size fifteen centuries ago? There is also the possibility that the 'mer' in Mercredesburn refers to the Saxon for lake, so we need a river site with a lake nearby, or alternatively, the 'Mercredaes' could have been a tribe, like the Haestingaes and this was a separate community that fought back fiercely. Frankish (French) influence exists at this time, so could it be possible that the river in question was Mercredi's bourne—Woden's river? Woden as a God was introduced by the Saxons and a powerful river may have been named in his honour. So unfortunately, we can't send a visitor to Sussex to the site of the Battle of Mercredesburn but hopefully here the determined visitor wanting to experience Saxon Sussex has some ideas.

Bosham - We start off back though in the west of the county. **1. Bosham**, south-west of Chichester, is not only perhaps the 'capital' of Sussex, if not a royal centre of power, but a voyage from it by Harold Godwinson in 1064 brought about the end of the Saxon Age. Having a monastery in the seventh century would have helped it become an important Saxon centre. Bosham's Church of the Holy Trinity has a Saxon tower from the time of Canute, and Alec Barr-Hamilton speculated it was Canute that ordered its building. Its Saxon features include a window that was once a doorway that goes nowhere and its magnificent chancel arch, the arch you walk under as you approach the altar. Pevsner called it 'one of the best Saxon arches in England'. Kings such as Canute and later Harold Godwinson had palaces there and its harbour was bustling, as the port of the Godwin estates. The Godwins were powerful overlords of Wessex, so it is apt that the village name is pronounced in the West Country-sounding 'Bozzum', but the Godwins were firmly of Sussex. The port was owned by the Godwin family and possibly the one from where they left to start their exile, ordered by Edward the Confessor and the port they returned to. Recent academic work has suggested that the majority of the nation's fleet of ships were based here too before 1066, making it the largest naval port in the country at that time. Bosham can also truly say it is a port that changed the course of British history as Harold Godwinson sailing from here in 1064 was the start of the fateful voyage to Normandy where he would be tricked or coalesced into giving his support to William of Normandy. His backtracking on this promise led to William's angry invasion of England and the subsequent battle between these two.

Invasion and raiding of Sussex was frequent from the 890s until the time of the Godwins, but before them the invaders were of Viking make-up, rather than Vikings who had settled in France for two centuries, which is what the Normans were. Bosham was the site of one raid by the earlier Norsemen where one of the church bells was carried off. A legendary story tells that the villagers rang the remaining bells and the stolen bell rang too, breaking through the bottom of the Viking ship and causing the Vikings to follow the bell to the bottom of the shore. The story continues that still today when the church bells in Bosham Church ring, the long-lost bell rings a solemn note in solidarity from the bottom of the sea. Quite how anyone has or can hear it is another matter! Despite the loss of a valuable bell and even after the destruction incurred during the Norman conquest, it was still registered in the Domesday Books (there were actually two) as one of the wealthiest ports in the country (its Saxon church appears in the Bayeux Tapestry too). This wealth isn't surprising as the base of the last of the Anglo-Saxon kings. It is believed by some historians that Harold was buried in the church at Bosham and escaped from the Battle of Hastings to fight a guerrilla war. The discovery of a grave that could reveal

Bosham Church

the answer whether Harold is buried at Bosham was investigated in 1954 but a request to open the grave properly to assess if it was Harold's grave was denied. Sussex may well still have its own 'Richard III moment' to look forward to, without the kerfuffle of having to dig up a car park either.

Bosham may have been the place of violence, but it also changed hands in the most peaceful of methods: via a kiss. The lands at Bosham transferred from the Archbishop of Canterbury to Earl Godwin, father of Harold by a cunning case of trickery—and probably a large pack of men waiting to rough up the religious leader! Godwin met the archbishop and asked, as people did then for the kiss of peace, by saying to the holy man the Latin words 'Da mihi basium'—give me peace. The archbishop would traditionally consent and give the kiss, which he did in this case. However, Godwin cheekily said he had asked instead for the lands of Bosham by saying 'Da mihi Boseam'—give me Bosham. He used his group of witnesses as proof that the archbishop had given him the Sussex Saxon port. Whatever Godwin had said, the lands were soon transferred to him and would belong to his family until taken off them by William the Conqueror. Harold Godwinson would receive a little more than a kiss planted on him this time—he traditionally is believed to have received an arrow in his eye and his body was torn to pieces.

Before Godwin's time Bosham was the place for numerous Saxon and Viking era legends. The story of Viking King Canute demonstrating his kingly powers still made him unable to hold back the oncoming tide is famously linked to the port and makes sense as a royal residence of the tenth and eleventh centuries. It is not Canute, who is buried in Winchester, but his daughter who provides us with another 'could have been buried here' story. His 8-year-old daughter is said to have drowned in the Roman Millstream and is buried under the steps at the foot of the chancel of the church. Whether this is true or not, Bosham is certainly a settlement with a regal past and a setting of the clashes over the centuries between the Saxons, the Vikings and the French descendants of Vikings, the Normans. It was the Southampton container port of its day, mixed with a Portsmouth naval base. As a port, it had no rival in the west of the county of Sussex—the fleet to protect these coasts sailed from either here or Pevensey—and it was the only port William the Conqueror personally kept in his control after 1066, perhaps due to how much he owed its previous owner in making him king. Bosham is also worth

Above: *Bosham Millstream*

Below: *Bosham Anchor Bleu*

a visit as it has the longest Christian history of any place in Sussex, and there are few places in England with a known earlier Christian settlement. For the fan of Britain's military past, Bosham's wealth and huge exposure to threats of invasion mean its defences were either very well removed or are waiting to be discovered. For these reasons, and as Sussex's foremost and last surviving coastal Saxon port, it is of huge historical significance.

Lunch locally: Bosham has a range of cafes and cosy pubs, the Anchor Bleu having the best view across the harbour. The cafe by the slip road called Breeze Coffee Shop and Tea Rooms to the harbour is the best to watch visitors to Bosham whose cars have been parked in the harbour pretend not to own them when they return and find them surrounded by the lapping waves. Even the drive in and out of Bosham provides a range of pubs such as the Bosham and the Millstream.

Just up the road from Bosham, and just as picturesque, is Dell Quay, another pretty Saxon port worth a visit, it is **Chichester** we again visit. It is 'visitworthy' (a new phrase I've just coined) not just as one of King Alfred's burhs (fortified sites and towns), which he ordered the rebuilding of, but as the site of one of the few battles in the country where the Saxons beat

Bosham High Tide

the Vikings in 894–895 AD and therefore the only Sussex site of a Viking defeat we know of. Earlier on when Sussex was a kingdom in its own right, it was the ancient capital of the kingdom of Sussex, something that we should celebrate more, much like Winchester celebrates its place as capital of Wessex. Chichester should also be celebrated as a Sussex survivor. It faced likely desolation after the Roman evacuation of Britain and would have been an empty ghost town of a site, with just animals living within its ruined walls and overgrown streets. Alfred's order to rebuild Cissa's camp (Chichester—the Saxon 'c' was pronounced 'ch') rejuvenated the town and ensured its walls became defensive for the first time in half a millennium. Being given the name of 'Cissa's Ceastre' suggests Aelle's son was a chieftain of the area after the Saxon's first battle in the 400s, but there is no evidence of him rebuilding Chichester's walls or leading the town. Cissa disappears out of the history books after his family's successful conquering of Pevensey in 491 AD, by which time Aelle had a complete and defensible kingdom. We don't even know if he succeeded his father in ruling Sussex or if Aelle's dynasty collapsed; the next record of Sussex kings being in the 600s. Nevertheless, the fact his name is attached to it suggests he probably utilized and occupied the site rather than sacking and burning the site as his family did with Pevensey. The lines of the Roman walls were certainly left, and if Aelle's base was on Seal's Island (Selsey), having a defensive site to defend his father north of that from invaders from the north made sense.

Unfortunately, establishing the story of Saxon Chichester does involve a lot of guesswork. Lack of archaeological remains means conjecture between Roman occupation and the time of Alfred. Our next mention in early Saxon (often referred to as the Pagan Saxon era) is when the Bishop of Selsey, Wilfrid (681–707) was given a 'certain parcel of land… in the southern part of Cicestriae, close to the sea with all the fields, meadows and rivers to it pertaining'. This charter, describing the gift of land from South Saxon King Ethelbert to Wilfrid suggests that the Saxon name for Chichester existed from at least this time, in the late seventh century.

Two centuries later in the 890s we know Chichester was rebuilt by Alfred, who would have wanted to celebrate the city's namesake as an early ancestor of his, the use of whose name would have reinforced his attempts to galvanize the now merged kingdoms of Wessex and Sussex as one against the Viking invaders at a time where 'Englaland' was increasingly looking as if it may become 'Daneland'. Alfred's rebuilding ready for the onslaught of 895–6 AD must have been substantial and well-planned as the burhware, the men of the burh that Alfred built on the Roman foundations, repulsed the Viking attack with several hundred murdered. The red drops on the city's coat of arms have been suggested to be the blood of the Viking leaders of the attack. Whatever the death toll, the fact that Alfred's rebuilding saved a settlement with few natural defences close to the shore is testament to the skill of the Saxon defenders or the anger at the Danish invaders.

With the ongoing threat from the Vikings continuing, it made sense to maintain the walls of the burh of Chichester, which is why the size of the town is reviewed in the Burghal Hidage document at the time of Edward the Elder (900–24), and the South Gate is mentioned in a charter in 930 AD, suggesting the defences are still seen as important. The Saxons mention 'Stanstrete' at this time, suggesting the Roman road is still in use, and Edward's successor Aethelstan had a mint in the town during his reign of 925–39 AD.

Money went hand in hand with religion at this time, so it is no surprise there is evidence of a Saxon monastery in Chichester by 956 AD during the reign of King Edwy, possibly called the Minster of St Peter, where the cathedral is now.

St Olave's Church - Our greatest evidence of religious Saxon Chichester that you can visit is **2. (The former) St Olave's Church**, tucked away in between the shops in North Street. You originally entered through an entrance to the south in Saxon times, rather than its later medieval west-facing entrance today and would have entered through a graveyard. You can see this entrance on turning right when you enter the building and the tall, narrow alcove is where the original Saxon entrance was in this building which dates back, it is believed, to between the 1030s and 1060s. St Olaf was a Norwegian king and later saint who sided with Ethelred the Unready against the Vikings and died in 1030, making the church Chichester's oldest. It is today a bookshop. By the time Olaf died in 1030, the integration of some Scandinavian settlers is evident by the way other

Chichester buildings nearby were owned by fellow Nordic merchants. Olaf was a busy man; helping keep Cnut (Canute) from becoming king of England in 1014 by his alliance with Ethelred and was also said to have pulled down London Bridge to help defeat his fellow countrymen. Whatever the truth in this, by the 1050s there was a cult of St Olaf across England with several churches, like this one, named after him. The existence of this church reminds us that the end of the Saxon Sussex era was also a time of Viking Sussex too.

Sussex without Satnav: Bosham to Chichester is an easy journey—once you come out of Bosham, take the A259 east back to Fishbourne and at the Fishbourne roundabout, cross the busy A27 and head into Chichester. Get on the ring road and park at the car park near the North Gate near the West Sussex Record Office, which is the best for walking down North Street towards St Olaves.

Burpham - Moving east to Worthing from Chichester, it is worth taking a detour off the A27 before you get to Crossbush so you can take the cul-de-sac to **3. Burpham**, one of Alfred's burhs and a lesser-known site most visitors to Sussex will never have heard of. The one road in and out ensures it is not on most people's travel plans, but as mentioned, it may well have been the site of the Battle of Mercredesburn. When you turn off the A27, you also get some of the most amazing views of Arundel, which itself is thought locally to have had a fortification built in Saxon times, although there is no evidence to support this. Today you can easily walk around the site of the burh and see the remains of its walls. The views are stunning and there is a playpark for the children to explore whilst you explore the past. There is no evidence of Burpham ever being involved in battles against the Vikings, and this peaceful nature is reflected today in the charming and peaceful village around the burh, which has had several famous inhabitants since the Saxons.

Lunch locally: Chichester has a wealth of cafes, pubs and restaurants. The George at Burpham is a busy and popular gastropub that is one of Sussex's finest inns. If the 'swipes' from Mitchell's Brewery in Steyning

George at Burpham

at the Frankland Arms in Washington were Belloc's favourite beer in the whole of Sussex, then my twenty-first century equivalent is a pint of Amber Eyes from the Greyhound Brewery in West Chiltington, which the George serves to perfection. You can also visit Nick and Sarah, the owners of the Greyhound at the Brewery and purchase this nectar from there, but my favourite experience of it was at the George.

We return to the first king of Sussex, or at least a tale attached to him with our next spot to visit. We have mentioned **Highdown** already, but it is the Saxon graveyard here supposedly of Sussex kings that brings us here once more. Aelle's contemporaries acknowledge his conquest of Sussex as the 'Bret-walder' (wide ruler), and indeed Sussex is wider than it is deep. They also credit his accomplishments in conquering other territories to the north and west of the county. This has provoked the question of whether it was Aelle who led the unsuccessful forces against a revitalized coalition of Brittonic forces at the Battle of Mount Badon somewhere in the west of England. The victorious opposing forces at Badon have been attributed to the 'Last Roman', Ambrosius Aurelianus, or even the leader later attributed to be King Arthur. Little is known about the timing, tactics or location of Badon and accounts differ, or ignore it altogether in the case of the *Anglo-Saxon Chronicle*, but it is thought to be sometime between 490–520 AD. This would make sense of Aelle leading the Saxon forces at Badon for that would have been by when his conquest of Sussex was complete with Sussex conquered. He would have been able to send his troops westwards to Badon and his defeat, if this was the case, might be due to his forces being fatigued after the Sussex campaign. It is also feasible for it to be in Aelle's lifetime if the 477 AD date for Aelle's family's arrival in England is accurate. Whatever the truth, it has been claimed that Aelle is one of the Saxon kings buried at Highdown, and so if it was him fighting at Badon against a resurgent force of Britons, it makes Highdown a lot more exciting to think it may be the burial place after the battle with someone who has been latterly called 'Arthur'. There is no certainty an Arthur of the Britons (by which we mean Welsh) existed, but there seems to be a memory of a successful leader taking on the Saxons at this time. Though unlikely, should by any chance any of this ever be found to be true, it would make a suitably dramatic death for the founder of the kingdom of Sussex.

So, what do we know of the cemetery at Highdown? It was created around 450 AD so may be too early for the Battle at Mount Badon. Chanctonbury was able to show its ancient past when its trees were uprooted, whereas Highdown's secrets were revealed by accident following the hill's owner, Edwin Henty (still celebrated in a nearby Ferring pub) deciding to plant trees within the hill fort in 1892. This would be unthinkable today, but perhaps he wanted to follow in the footsteps of Chanctonbury Ring planter Charles Goring a few miles away. Before a full excavation could begin Henty discovered the workmen involved in the planting had lost or stolen some of the finds. The rest of the finds were still incredible however; a total of eighty-six Anglo-Saxon graves. The losses were still to continue though: the sharing of the skeletons between local museums wasn't greatly organized and led to a large number of these also becoming lost. Victorian archaeologists and antiquarians were not always as professional in their excavations or organization as they could have been.

To walk where these were, start within the camp as most of the graves were inside here, only a few graves existed outside the outline of the old hill fort. These graves were all from a relatively similar period so this graveyard was only in use for a short time, suggesting this was the burial site after a major battle. The fact the skeletons were mostly male, of 6ft in height, buried with weapons and in early adulthood suggests also they were warriors and they died in some of the earliest Saxon attacks, but some questions still need answering. We do not know whether these men died defending or attacking Highdown, or whether they died in a nearby battle. Some remains were buried, others cremated, so prompting us to ask if they were killed in two different events with different burial traditions, whether they were some Saxons and some Britons or whether some of them died in flames as a wooden fort at Highdown was torched. This burial could well predate the suspect *Anglo-Saxon Chronicle*'s given date of 477 AD for Aelle's invasion, as does other archaeological evidence, thus also making us ask why the *Chronicle* was so definite in its dating. Whatever the answers to these questions, the people burying these warriors at Highdown wanted them to be seen and remembered—there would have been markers for these graves originally and they were buried on a busy Saxon 'motorway'—near the crossroads of two busy and ancient trackways.

They were wealthy too—jewellery such as beads, amber, rings and brooches were buried with them, along with glass vessels, brooches, buckles, porcelain and, most mysteriously, flattened bronze tubes whose purpose was never established. How they looked must have concerned some of them in life as tweezers were also found.

It is not the period of unsettlement in the 400s as the Saxons conquered that leaves us with the most to visit and celebrate, it is their period of settlement from the 500s onwards. The Saxon half-century of conquest gives us our settlements with military beginnings; the 'burhs' leaving us with Bury, Chanctonbury, Cissbury, Burpham and Bramber (Bram-burh) to name a few. However, we have a much wider range of settlements that celebrate the earliest Saxon chieftains who settled once the conquest was over—those ending in 'ing' such as Lancing, Steyning, Sompting, and those with 'ham' as their suffix suggest farming communities—Shoreham, Stopham, Selham. Later community names as the Saxon era progresses celebrate the descendants of these earlier chieftains surviving, or perhaps a more collective approach to ruling. The suffix 'ing' of the earlier settlements is replaced by 'ington': 'the place of the sons/people of'. This gives us the later settlement names such as Washington, Sullington, and Durrington. Despite waves of Viking invasions from the 800s to 1066, the fightback by Alfred and entrenchment of the Saxons meant Scandinavian impact to the county is minimal today. We recognize our county today as vaguely the same as the Saxons; Romans travelling just a few centuries forward in time would not have recognized theirs.

This wealth of Saxon sites means we are spoilt for choice, but at the same time limited in our chances to see much of Saxon architecture as most building they did was wood and thatch, wattle and daub. The stone Norman churches we see are often built on the site of the ashes of Viking destruction of Saxon predecessors. This means a Saxon county has relatively little to show from the fifth to the eleventh centuries. Our exploration of Saxon sites will be dominated by their churches or Saxon remains in churches. Visitors to Sussex seeking the Saxon era may want to gain a greater understanding of Saxon history through the very different geography of the county then however. It is incredible just how different Saxon Sussex would have looked a millennium and more back. The coastline was generally further south at this time in West Sussex, whereas East Sussex saw the sea encroach far greater inland than it does today so that Rye, Pevensey and New Winchelsea all had salt water lapping against them. West Sussex had a very different coastline with Selsey practically an island, which projected much further out to the south-west. Saxon Selsey, including the landing beach of Aelle, Cymensora are now well and truly covered by the English Channel. All the rivers were wider and reached far further inland, matched by a higher water table. Fortified medieval castles such as Amberley and Bodiam were being built as invaders could still get easily that far inland and attack inland settlements over half a millennium later. The sea touched upon Burpham, Bramber, presented a widewater lagoon or broadwater as far inland as Broadwater today in Worthing (hence the name) and effectively making Worthing an eerie salt-water surrounded peninsula at high tide. Higher water levels made the bridges needed at Beeding and Lewes much wider; floodplains were silver inland seas at places like Pulborough for

Washington

much of the year and even places like **4. Washington**, equidistant between Arun and Adur, were sat above much wetter and deeper networks of waterways. This made Washington, a small village today bypassed by roads as well as waterways, an important Saxon headquarters until the Normans replaced it with the new or at least revamped burh at Bramber, which was by a mightier waterway, the Adur.

It is hard to envisage Washington in the present day as a place of some importance with its population of just 2,000 people; only a few hundred of which are within the boundaries of the village today rather than the parish. Yet Washington was more important than Horsham by the time of the Domesday Books, controlling manor lands seven miles north and even possibly as far away as Gatwick. Washington, although perched on the side of a hill, was no military defensive site but like Steyning, sites further away from the coast prospered in Saxon times. As the Adur silted up and its waterway narrowed, the port at Old and then eventually New Shoreham (Shoreham-by-Sea) replaced the port at Steyning, St Cuthman's Port, which today it is even hard to find. Washington has little physical evidence to alert us to its Saxon past except for its name, but the site of the church and Church Farm next door suggest where this Saxon settlement existed. There is some evidence of a court being held at the manor house that is Church Farm, and the Norman church of St Mary's at Washington replaced no doubt a Saxon one on that site. One major clue as to the age of Washington is the ancient drovers' road through the village which burrows

View towards Lower Chancton Farm where Saxon silver was discovered, near Washington

down through the hillside Washington is on. The other was the find in 1866 of nearly 3,000 pieces of Anglo-Saxon silver in nearby Chancton Farm, believed to be buried by a Saxon off to fight the Normans at Hastings. Should you wish to see where a number of these coins were traded in beer, then you can try the Frankland Arms, also beloved by Hilaire Belloc who sung the praises of its 'swipes' (beer) in his early twentieth century book *The Four Men*.

Sussex without satnav: As we've done before, take the A280 back up to the A27 and head east until Offington Road roundabout, left up the A24 to Washington. Steyning, our next location, is just east along the A283 out of Washington along a scenic but sometimes dangerous route, with an S-bend that has caused many a speeding or unfocussed driver to end up closer to nature than they would have wished.

5. Steyning we have mentioned before when we visited Hill Brow but this time we visit the town below the camp and for a more peaceful visit. According to folklore, Steyning was established due to the travels of St Cuthman, an eighth century West Country boy who could keep sheep within an area just by drawing a circle in the ground with his staff. His sheep may have stayed still but Cuthman didn't when his father died, forcing the family into poverty. The saint-to-be took to the road in a do-it-yourself wheelbarrow to find a

new home after their few belongings had all been sold. Begging on the road
must have taken its toll on Cuthman's temper and when field hands gathering
in hay laughed at the barrow breaking he supposedly caused rain to fall on
their harvest, which it apparently did for many subsequent years. The same
problem with his barrow a few miles later led to Cuthman deciding it was a
sign to stop and make a new home. This home was to be Steyning and once
he had built a shelter for his mother by the harbourside he set about building
a church at the site where St Andrew's Church is today. This wooden
church nearly collapsed the stories tell, until apparently God himself helped
straighten a collapsing timber. The fame of these events spread far and wide
and led people to visit Steyning on pilgrimages after his death. Steyning
even became known as St Cuthman's Port.

An even greater Saxon link, again involving a parent though, should
bring visitors to the town. Not only was Steyning part of the royal burh of
Bramber and one of the Saxon mints, it was the place of burial of a Saxon
king. King Ethelwulf of Wessex, none other than the father of King Alfred
the Great was buried at Steyning church. This was as he had left the western
part of the kingdom of Wessex in the hands of his son, Ethelbald, when he

The Church of St Andrew and St Cuthman, Steyning

went overseas and Ethelbald refused to hand it back on his Father's return. This meant Ethelwulf was only left with Kent and Sussex, so Steyning seems to have become a temporary capital, a bit like Bonn in Iron Curtain-divided Germany. Still today we are reminded of the fact that it was the centre of a royal estate by the fact there is a King's Barn in the town. Royalty has mostly deserted Steyning ever since, much as the Adur has, Bramber instead being visited by royals. Even Ethelwulf was eventually moved and reburied in the capital of Winchester when Ethelbald died and his next son, Ethelbert, took control of all of Wessex again. Ethelwulf must have been forgiving of Ethelbald, however, as he left West Wessex, which Ethelbald had refused to return in life, to him in his will. Steyning folk today are equally forgiving and friendly, compared to some other similar towns. This might be as they live in such a charming and historic town. A second church was built on Cuthman's site, at the end of the Saxon era during Edward the Confessor's reign (1042–1066 AD) and the current church is late Norman. It has the feel of a small French cathedral and an amazing sense of calm reigns inside. It also has a double-incised coffin slab which is said to be the coffin slab of either Ethelwulf or Cuthman. Steyning has one last link to the Saxon era: it helped bring about its demise. Edward the Confessor granted the royal estates to the Abbey of Fecamp in Normandy. Regaining these lands from Harold Goodwineson after his coronation was a small but solid reason for William of Normandy to justify his invasion of Saxon England.

Lunch Locally: Steyning's eateries have already been highlighted, but nearest to the church is the wonderful Norfolk Arms in Church Street, where you feel more like you're drinking in someone's front room. The building hides a marvellous Tudor staircase.

St Mary at Sompting - Churches are the best architectural examples of Saxon architecture we can touch and there are many other churches in Sussex with Saxon remains. The list includes Lyminster, Sullington, Botolphs, Bolney, Old Shoreham and Clayton but there are two which are most worthy of a visit. Worth is one of them, but the most famous, and perhaps our most famous Saxon building altogether in Sussex, is the church of **6. St Mary at Sompting**. If there was an award for our greatest Saxon architectural treasure then St Mary's would win it; not just as a rare survivor of the Saxon Age, not because it is fifty years older than other Saxon remains in Sussex but because it is so architecturally unique in this country. What makes it this is its unique four-sided gabled spire above its tower, which is referred to as a pyramidal 'cap'. The only other example, now lost, was at St Benet's church in Cambridge until the early 1800s. This spire design is called 'Rhenish Helm' and reminds us of the Germanicism of our invaders from this era; this design being found especially along the Rhine in north-east Germany. It is simplistic compared with later elaborate church spires but still a work of art; especially when you consider this: the four diamond-shaped faces of the tower have watched over Sompting and the more-recent Worthing for 1,100 years. These four diamonds join together to form a pyramid and each side of the tower uniquely has a rhomboid shape pointing upwards. It translates as 'Rhineland Helmet', which is the nearest you get to a *Men Behaving Badly*-style gag with church architecture.

The exterior gets better though. The tower dates from the tenth century but has Roman bricks if you look closely, which were probably recycled from the site at Park Brow. Despite its age, there is something of the

The Church of St Mary at Sompting

automaton about it; it has echoes of early Cold War rockets pointing at the sky. It could be one of the Thunderbirds in stone camouflage. The main body of the church was also built by the romantic order of the Knights Templar, who had their own little chapel within—architecturally could this building get any sexier? Unlike most Saxon buildings remaining, the church at Sompting has architectural treasures not just inside, but these are worth a look. Like Bosham, the church has a magnificent tower arch, elaborately decorated but not as grand in scale. It is deliciously off-centre which adds to the slightly haphazard and almost frail charm of the building; you wonder how this church and slender tower has survived the centuries. The back of a blocked doorway also has Saxon carvings, as there also is in the chancel. Sompting's church is one that certainly makes you look up, and so it should; it is believed it was once 25ft taller and the tower was reduced in height in the 1760s. St Mary's may be shorter than it once was, but this internationally-famous church still reminds us of the achievement of our Germanic ancestors. No wonder it is Grade I listed.

Sussex without satnav: Steyning to Sompting involves a spectacular drive over the Downs which you access from the road out of Steyning towards Bramber. As you have nearly left the town, there is an old white signpost pointing right which says 'Steyning/To the bostal'. Take this road for a spectacular drive or walk—which takes you past Hill Brow which we mentioned earlier. Bostal is itself a Saxon word unique to Sussex (Beor-stiege) which means 'steep road up a hill' so you are getting the genuine Saxon Sussex experience here! Despite being in Sompting, St Mary's is divided by the busy A27 from the pubs in the village, so it may be worth eating in Steyning first; otherwise you have a long-winded 180° drive to pubs such as the Marquess of Granby or The Gardeners Arms.

Worth - Our last visit in West Sussex is in a rural location a short hop from the bustling near-city of Crawley. In fact, Crawley has crept outwards to the east so much that it has swallowed up what was once the parish of Worth, a fact some residents still resent. Borders of the parish have not only changed; Nairn and Pevsner in their wonderful *The Buildings of England* logged it firmly under East Sussex. Villages at one point when signs were changed to say 'Pound Hill and Worth', would cross out the 'Pound Hill' bit, refusing to be lumped in with the encroaching younger upstart. This may be to do with one of the jewels in the Saxon Sussex crown, the wonderful **7. Worth Church**, or St Nicholas' Church to give it its full title.

Worth is a church to be proud of; again, one of the oldest in the country. Like Sompting, parts of it have been dated from 950–1050 AD but what makes it more mysterious than St Mary's is that it would have been built surrounded by a forest at the time; the name of the village means clearing. It is incredible to think how this mini-cathedral would have looked to a Saxon traveller coming across it out of dense Wealden forests. The size and location suggest that it had had some other purpose, but we know not what—if it was the place of prayer for royals using the hunting park nearby as has been suggested, then we must be missing perhaps a sumptuous royal residence nearby. What makes Worth even worthier architecturally is that it doesn't seem to have changed from the original Saxon floor plan. Building a stone church at this point in time is exceedingly rare—the Saxons mostly built in wood or wattle and daub so this suggests again that Worth was worth something—only royalty or the very highest in the land would have commissioned such a building—especially if it was a standalone building with no accompanying palace or manor house. What if it was just erected for a very special event—a royal wedding, perhaps? Alex Barr-Hamilton has an equally enchanting theory in *In Saxon Sussex* that it could be the faithful rebuilding of a Roman building on this spot. Our only other clue is that the River Mole starts near here, so perhaps Roman settlers followed the Mole up from the Thames (which it joins) and built a church in the area where the river started. Inside, it has a 22ft high chancel arch that has been described as the greatest of its kind in England. So Worth makes us ask 'Why here?', 'Why so early?', 'Why so big?', 'Why on its own?', 'What was it for?' and makes us utter, when we get inside, simply 'Wow!'

Sussex without Satnav: From Sompting, head east along the A27 (this might be why you might want to eat in Steyning first) and continue until it joins the A23. Head north until you reach Nymans and take the B2110 (if the A23 has become the M23 you've gone too far, although the church is just a few hundred metres off the M23). Follow the B2110 until the B2036 is on your left and then take this until you reach Street Hill and then Church Road, turning right both times.

It is the Vikings that provide the final act in the grand and lengthy drama that is the era of Saxon Britain. This is due to the French Viking expats that finally won the two centuries-long battle between Saxons and Scandinavia, with the Normans conquering Britain. Therefore, it is only right we explore the Viking impact on Sussex. The Vikings never dominated and settled in Sussex as they did in other parts of the country, especially in the Danelaw, the north-east part of England Alfred the Great allowed Guthrum to keep under the Treaty of Wedmore. The greatest impact of the Vikings is in East Sussex (or at least Brighton and Hove) as Hove is a Viking word, which explains its difference to the sea of Saxon place names surrounding it. Brighton also has the 'Knabb' where the Pump House is today, a Scandinavian word for hill, which is not too different from the unfortunately-named Saxon derivative, 'knob', which does exist in places in West Sussex, such as Baldwin's Knob, near Loxwood. Another Viking and Saxon word that has also had an impact in the west of Sussex is 'Steine', meaning stoney place or ground. Brighton's Old Steine seems to have used the name first, with West Sussex settlements of Bognor and Worthing using the name much later too to denote a green area, rather than a stoney ground. Worthing's Steyne is spelt with a 'y' just to be difficult but the area was originally called Springers or Stringers.

There is one other place in West Sussex that reminds us of the Viking invasions. **8. Kingly Bottom**, near Chichester, is named, according to Harrison Ainsworth in *Ovingdean Grange*, due to the battle between Saxons and Danes that took place there. Yew trees tend to be planted to protect the dead in graveyards and cemeteries and the yews in Kingly Bottom, or Kingly Vale, are equally apt as they are said to mark a victory of Chichester men over a party of marauding Danes in 900, and that the dead were buried beneath the barrows on the hill—the Devil's Humps we mentioned earlier. Could it be they acquired their name as the Danes were seen as Devils to the Saxons who buried them? It is accessible today as part of the Kingly Vale National Nature Reserve—we will revisit it during the chapter on Civil War Sussex as it is 'kingly' for another reason too. So, apart from these postscripts, in terms of names or architecture, the Vikings would have little long-lasting impact on Sussex. Their descendants, however, after a two-century detour via Normandy, would have the biggest and longest-lasting impact of any group of invaders to this county and would provide the most significant event Sussex is known for in the history books.

CHAPTER 4

Norman Sussex

Should you wish to explore a tour of the Norman Conquest, then you start this side of the Channel, south-west of Chichester at **1. Bosham**. As mentioned earlier, it was the royal Saxon port owned by the Godwins that played a dual role in the Norman invasion. By the time Cnut lived or visited his suspected palace there, links were already in existence between Normandy and the English court. Ethelred the Unready had spent time in exile there and his family had married into the Duchy of Normandy. He had given English land to Normandy long before the Normans seized it all after 1066. As the Danes who had attacked southern England had been repulsed by Alfred, they had found easier conquest in France. Kings of England in the eleventh century needed treaties with the Normans as they tended to harbour wandering Viking fleets, being more or less cousins a few generations removed from their Norse brethren. It was better to keep

Quay Meadow, Bosham

Normandy sweet. This may have been why Harold Godwinson made his fateful voyage to his soon-to-be nemesis, William of Normandy in 1064, or it may have been to do with trade—the Channel wasn't much of a barrier to commerce at this time. The other theory is that he was shipwrecked there. Whichever way, Bosham remains relevant in Norman England, as a feature on the Bayeux Tapestry, as a place that remained a bustling port, but as the place that started the short-term chain of events which led to a different royal family leading England and dominating Sussex for the next century. Their descendants are still on the throne today. The Vikings finally came to rule the country they had raided, invaded and battered for two centuries. Norman Sussex is Norsemens' Sussex, we must remember, and so Norman architectural styles, laws, hierarchy, religious dominance and even building materials would all be imposed on the county. Sussex would never look the same again.

Of course, the invasion of Sussex was famously in the eastern part of the county, so we will have to wait for the next volume of *Visitors' Historic Britain* for that. There are no records of particular rebellions against William in Sussex after Hastings, and this was probably as most Sussex noblemen and landlords would have been linked to Harold and drafted into the battle as last-minute reinforcements. The different manors became leaderless; which helps explain nearly all Sussex manors being in non-Saxon hands by the time of the Domesday Books. Some historians have tried to argue that there was a second invasion fleet that landed at Chichester, similar to the theory that Aelle had a second, reserve invasion Saxon attack fleet using Shoreham as reinforcements, but this has never been proven. Some suggested Norman routes show a westerly advance across Sussex but William's priority once battle was won was to subdue Kent and then capture London. William amazingly managed this despite his small and now further reduced invasion force, and with the much-forgotten and far stronger claimant to the throne, Edgar the Aetheling, residing within London's walls. But Sussex would feel the force of the Normans; it was the gateway to the country the Normans had used to enter it from their territory. William had enemies in France as Normandy was but one province—that gateway needed to be rebuilt and reinforced. This meant Sussex rivers needed to be monitored and defended as potential speedy inroads to the capital William newly controlled. They were also the borders of the existing 'roped off' areas (or 'rapes' as they came to be known) that the Saxons had divided Sussex into. William strengthened these subdivisions of this gateway territory and these five (later six) rapes would each be given to a trusted lieutenant to monitor, raise funds from and protect by building a castle on, usually by the main river on its border.

This meant the first priority was the building of Norman castles, which was mostly the rebuilding of Anglo-Saxon burhs. This is where we start our exploration of Norman Sussex. Once control was gained of each rape and its north-south route, with a castle watching for potential invasion and internal invasion, as well as protecting garrisons of Norman troops, then a different business could start. That business was the thanking of God for the successful outcome of the invasion and battle and asking for penance for the lives taken. Security would be first, spiritual needs second; churches and cathedrals would follow castles. We start our exploration of castles with the one furthest west, but also the largest rape originally (until it was split into two. Roger de Montgomery originally controlled both **2. Chichester** and Arundel). Chichester remained an important port and it seems having a fortified town nearby continued as Sussex ports were crucial due to their proximity to the lands in Normandy; the English Channel was a busy motorway for trade between the two main lands in this cross-channel enterprise. A motte-and-bailey was thrown up in the north-east corner of the city in what is now Priory Park today. This remains the best place in the city to see not just the medieval guildhall but the city walls, the motte the Norman fort once stood on, and the gallant cathedral all at once. Later, by the twelfth century, this temporary structure was replaced by a stone structure, but so completely was it removed after being captured by the French in the little-known invasion of 1216–17 that strangely, no signs remain. It is hard to imagine in this peaceful park today with cricketers bowling and children playing that Saxons would have been enslaved cruelly to build this mound. Equally, your imagination needs help to envisage 150 years later a vicious fight between the French Prince Louis' forces and loyalists to King John defending the castle.

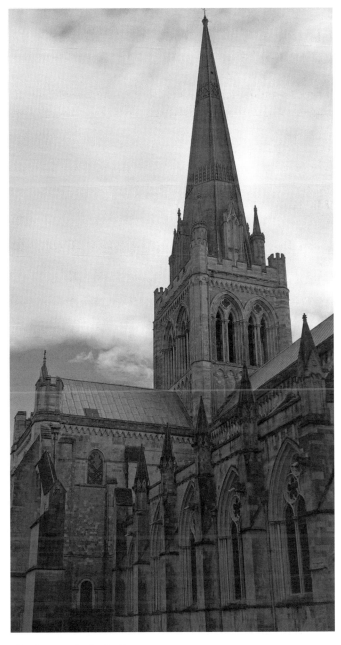

Chichester Cathedral

3. Chichester Cathedral - It's hard to dislike any cathedral. A cathedral that has survived over 900 years and witnessed its spire collapsing, that has architectural additions from nearly every major era period from the Normans and is the country's only medieval cathedral that can be seen from the sea, makes it a wonder to behold. Essentially it is the construction of Bishop Ralph Luffa, Bishop of Chichester who had the lengthy tenure of 1091 to 1123, responsibility of replacing the Saxon cathedral at Selsey. It is unusual for cathedrals of that era as it was erected using stone transported from the Isle of Wight rather than Caen, which was the Norman tradition. Its first test of survival was not long after building in 1187 when it faced a series of horrific fires. This would cause problems centuries later as the rebuilding recycled the fire-damaged and weakened stone, which led to weaknesses in the surviving building. The 277ft-high spire, which was added somewhere between the late 1200s or early 1300s, then presented the cathedral's next challenge when it collapsed in a storm that lasted several days in 1861, despite the valiant efforts of cathedral workmen high up on the roof. Only five years later, a new replica spire was back in place, thanks to the work of Sir Gilbert Scott, and so sailors passing by could once again use it as a navigation aid. It appears the builders were aided in finding the right spot for the cathedral by an even earlier religious group of buildings that were on the site before. If all the above doesn't persuade you to visit

Chichester Cathedral

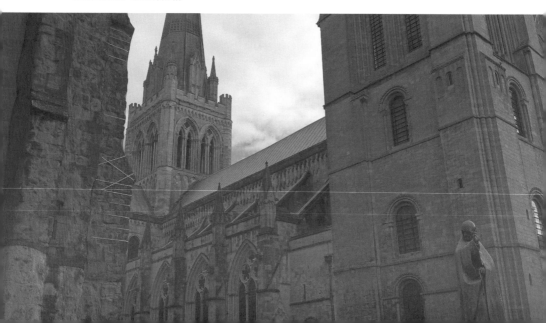

Chichester Cathedral, then its bell tower might. Chichester is unique as the only cathedral city in England where the bell tower is separate from the actual cathedral, being located 30ft away from the north-east entrance. Two of its bells have been ringing since Tudor times (not non-stop!) and it is still possible to climb to the top to see the views. The cathedral gardens are equally magnificent and, unusually, you can actually stay in a holiday property in the cathedral grounds.

Church Norton - Returning back to Chichester Harbour, we have a mysterious extra defensive site that seems to have been a lookout post in Norman times. On the south-western side of Pagham Harbour at **4. Church Norton** south of St Wilfrid's Chapel there is a Norman Ringwork defence of a large semi-circular mound and ditch around its front and sides. It is believed that this hosted a large wooden tower and must have had some longevity as it was used as a lookout post at the time of the Spanish Armada. It is known as the Mound, or the Mount and is a restricted English Heritage site, but can be seen from the footpath that leads to the harbour at Pagham. It may be this site tells of more than one era as excavations have led to evidence of possible Iron Age occupation. Likewise, Neolithic evidence was also found during excavations. Even more exciting, Roman remains found may mean this was once the site of a villa and the site may be Anglo-Saxon too. Half of the site is unfortunately under the site of the church, so we may never fully know though. The area itself had an interesting time under the Normans. The centre of Christianity in Sussex was moved to Chichester by the French invaders from Selsey in this era, so St Wilfrid's was later reduced in size from a grand structure to a chapel, with its structure mostly removed to Selsey and rebuilt there. This does leave Church Norton with an air of peacefulness today which leaves us able to image its important past throughout different eras.

Sussex without Satnav: Church Norton and Pagham Harbour are best to visit along with Bosham we mentioned first in this chapter, and then go up to Chichester and Midhurst. The route is longer than you'd expect though due to the watery channels of the harbour getting in your way. Take Bosham and Walton Lanes out of Bosham to the main road (the A259) which you stay on heading south-easterly as it becomes the A27 past the south of Chichester (don't go into Chi, but take the A286 and then B2201 south to Selsey). The Selsey Road becomes Chichester Road and you need finally the B2145 to Rectory Lane — Pagham is just east of Selsey.

Midhurst - Should invaders in the early years of Norman reign, or a Saxon insurrection have battled their way past Chichester, then another castle guarded the road north at St Anne's Hill above the river valley at Midhurst. This became known as **5. Bohun, or Midhurst Castle** after the de Bohun family who were later given this estate, and built on what seems to be existing Saxon defences, although there are no records of Alfred or his successors having a burh here. The now-wooded hill was the site first of a motte-and-bailey defence soon after the Norman arrival, but apparently not until after 1086 as it fails to appear in the Domesday Books. Like other inland castles in Sussex, it was built to further strengthen the Normans' hold on this vital county which could be used by invaders once more and so was vital to retain strict vigilance over. It is hard to visualize today, due to the heavy tree coverage surrounding, but its lofty hilltop position meant it could ensure invaders weren't using the (then navigable) River Rother, just as Pulborough Castle guarded the deeper reaches of the Arun. Like many other castles, it caused the town it guarded and watched over to develop, with roads such as Church Hill and Edinburgh Square seeming to support the castle. The Rother was crucial in those days to the wealth of the country as used for trade and commerce as roads through the impoverished lands of the Weald could be impassable in the winter months.

It was built originally with wood and earthworks, like many at the time, and it seems the earlier Saxon defence ditch was filled in by the fourteenth century. It (unusually) had two baileys, one on top of the hill, and one on the western side. Stone walls and buildings were in place by the twelfth century, the foundations of which can still be seen today. The later building was constructed on land owned by Barons by that time known as the de Bohuns who had been granted the land by Richard I and within the grounds of the castle they built a St Anne's chapel, which gives the hill its name today. (The hill has also been known as Thanes Hill, according to an 1872 guidebook, which seems to be a corruption of 'St Anne's'). The castle was demolished apparently by the Bohuns when they moved from either this building or their manor house to the building that would eventually become Cowdray. By the safer Tudor era, the only castle building was coastal defences built during the reign of Henry VIII, so Cowdray was a luxurious manor rather than a fortified building. The castle was apparently demolished by the Bishop of Durham at some point between 1284 and 1311. It may only have foundations left but an exploration of its grounds today means you get to explore one of the county's historic and much-forgotten castle sites.

Sussex without Satnav: Midhurst is up the A286 from the ring road in Chichester and easily signposted. Midhurst tends to be a town people easily drive through. For the castle site, park in the town's library grounds or near the church and Spread Eagle Hotel for a cross-century exploration of the town. From Midhurst to Arundel, take the A272, B2138, and the A29. The route into Arundel from the north via the A29 takes you directly to the castle.

Lunch locally: You can combine both of these in Midhurst with the excellent Spread Eagle Hotel, which we mention later in the Tudor Sussex section. Midhurst has a range of good cafes and pubs in the High Street too, such as The Angel, well-known for its steaks. From the castle, a short drive for a mile takes you to the waterside Black Rabbit pub, where you can gaze in the direction of both the castle and towards Burpham, so seeing two defensive settlements at once. There are a wealth of pubs, cafes and restaurants in the High Street in Arundel, or the King's Arms in Tarrant Street is worth a detour.

6. Arundel Castle Construction of these castles, and reconstruction rather of Saxon burhs, led, as it had with Alfred's burh-building, to the development of towns, the creation of new towns, and thus roads developing between them. Intersections of these roads led to the need for further new settlement developments, and so Norman Sussex is an era of further progress in the development and infrastructure of the county. The protection of a castle and the trade possible with it were strong incentives for towns to develop in their shadow. This is largely the case with Arundel which, although there are claims it had Saxon defences, this could be confusion with Burpham's existing burh, or perhaps a late Saxon-era burh that replaced Burpham, to the west of the Arun. Whatever the case here, Arundel has evidence of possible prehistoric earthworks where Arundel Castle is, as well as Roman remains suggesting it was home at least to a Roman or pre-Roman nobleman. By the time of the conquest there was probably a small port at Arundel as Alfred had left the land in his will in 901 AD and there was apparently a minster church by late Saxon times. Nevertheless, the declaration of Arundel as a separate rape from that of Chichester and the construction of the castle by Roger de Montgomery around 1067 speeded up the development of the town and Burpham was slowly neglected. Arundel Castle today has its eleventh century keep on the site of the original Norman motte-and-bailey that de Montgomery built. The keep was built between 1070 and 1090. There are no Norman windows to look for, but the south side has a Norman doorway, now blocked. For other Norman parts of the castle, look for the eleventh century Sussex flint walls and two early castle windows that are now blocked. Something else to look out for is a banner flown from the well tower in the Norman keep. This means the Duke of Norfolk is in residence.

Arundel Castle

Sussex without Satnav: You can take the faster A27 and head north on the A283 at the Adur flyover if you want to follow the Adur northerly, as perceived invaders of Bramber would have done. This gives you an impressive view of the castle as you cross the 1981 bridge over the river. The castle's remains from its gatehouse are lit up at night, making it more evocative. Alternatively, for a slower and more breathtaking view, avoid the Upper Beeding bypass and travel slowly on the ancient road through Beeding (as Upper Beeding is known) across the old bridge to Bramber, and you'll see the castle remains slowly loom up above you as you approach. An alternative is the more scenic, but increasingly busy, A29/A283 route from Arundel via Houghton, Amberley, Storrington, Steyning and then Bramber. This is one of the more dangerous of Sussex's roads, but you come quicker to the castle which is approached through a tight gateway to the west of Bramber village on the Bramber/Steyning/Maudlin Lane roundabout. The drive up to the car park at the castle is steep and can be slippery, so this presents a good opportunity to leave the car at Shoreham and cycle up to Bramber using the Downs Link cycle path along this pretty stretch of the Adur.

7. Bramber Castle may only have a motte, gatehouse and a few ruined walls left but it is a wonderfully moving place to visit, that still feels every bit a Norman castle if you close your eyes and engage your imagination. The old walls can be easily traced, the views are spectacular, and you can see the time when the Adur lapped against the castle's foundations and a keep stood proudly on top of the motte watching out for invaders. Although the castle's heyday was at the time of the Normans, it was likely to have been a Saxon burh, (defensive site), hence the Saxon name of Bram-burh.

William de Braose, who had fought with William of Normandy was given thirty-eight Sussex manors by his king for his service, and was ordered to build the castle controlling his lands from the castle, replacing the likely Saxon burh there. This seat became a powerful centre of power in the days before the Adur silted up and narrowed. Shoreham would eventually replace it as the main harbour on the river but before that the family controlling it were seen as one of the most powerful in the land. Bramber ended up having its stone mostly used to build local roads. Today, with a wall of the gatehouse standing tall as the only remnant of this once-mighty castle, it is almost as if Bramber cocks a middle finger up at the centuries defying it to become ruined further.

Lunch Locally: Bramber has the Toll House Best Western which has a popular carvery as well as hotel rooms. Bramber has an Indian restaurant and also the Castle Inn, which serves great food. Beeding, across the bridge, has the King's Head and the Rising Sun. In the other direction, Steyning has the other pubs and cafes mentioned earlier.

If Bohun Castle at Midhurst was built to ensure invasions that passed Chichester were stopped further inland up the Arun, **8. Knepp Castle** must have fulfilled the same role for Bramber, protecting the Wealden route northwards. Like Bohun Castle, it requires the power of imagination (or time travel) but the remaining stump of a castle on top of a motte was once abreast of a much wider and navigable Adur, that is now mostly marshy land with a tiny trickle of a stream. Even as recently as 1530 the tidal Adur lapped up to the castle grounds, even though the mouth of the river was still thirteen miles to the south then. This would have presumably been the way the now cleared stones for building the castle were transported as during the 1100s timber from the forests at Knepp was transported by river as far as Southampton. A basic road north also existed along what is now the A24 although it was not a proper road between Worthing and here at West Grinstead until the early 1800s. The need for ground-down stone for this eventual turnpike road seems to explain why the castle was so nearly completely ruined by the late 1700s. At its peak though, this was the hunting lodge as well for Bramber, which King John used five times when he wasn't arguing with his barons or murdering his nephew. He wasn't the first king of England to do so; Historic England states that 'King William was known to have visited Knepp several times for hunting.' This was probably as it, along with Bramber, was constructed both by William's son-in-law, another William, de Braose. The most apt description is that it looks like 'a broken tooth', and there is indeed little to see here today, but the walks around here are glorious, with the Chanctonbury part of the Downs majestically rising in the distance, the wonderful Knepp Park to explore and Kneppmill Pond as well as Sussex writer Hilaire Belloc's windmill, used for the series

Knepp Castle

Jonathan Creek in nearby Shipley. Kneppmill Pond, which we mention later, has been described as one of the most beautiful stretches of water in Sussex due to its size, settings and views.

The 30ft-high castle stump is technically 'Old Knepp Castle', although the current Knepp Castle is about as much a castle as Roy Castle was, but it is still pretty as you'd expect from a design by Nash, who also designed the Royal Pavilion in Brighton. Mock castles are always a joy though, and it is a shame the building was so ravaged by fire in 1904. The new 'castle' is in private hands, but the grounds are opened up in an annual event and can be used for Sussex safaris. We will revisit Old Knepp slightly later when it becomes what seems like John's favourite hunting lodge (although there is a place with nearly that name in the West Country!) in the early Middle Ages. There is disagreement over the origins of its name; the family that owned it believed it was a reference to a French phrase for its proximity to the flatness of the millpond but there is no evidence that existed before the 1300s. It is more likely to be a similar version of 'Knabb', the word for hill, or 'Cnapp', the crest of a hill, which the castle sat on. According to *Castles in Sussex* by John Guy, it has also been called 'Knob'. Not a name these days you'd want for an edifice designed to terrify others. Or perhaps it is. The ruins are deceiving in that like the motte they sit on, they appear as if they were part of a circular building, but they are in fact what was left of a rectangular keep.

Sussex without satnav: It's back along the A283 for you, valued visitor—to Washington, which can be a good place to base yourself for exploring West Sussex either at the campsite or in one of its B & Bs. From the village that once had Hilaire Belloc's favourite beer, head north up the A24 again. Knepp is a walk from Shipley or Dialpost, both just off the A24. After Knepp, if you're moving onto Edburton Hill, then back down the A24 to Washington, A283 to Upper Beeding and park at High Trees car park (which doesn't have any high trees in it, bizarrely!) From here, you can walk along the South Downs Way to Edburton. The village of Edburton is below it and is another route with less of a walk.

Lunch Locally: If you're coming up from Worthing up the A24 northwards, you can stop for lunch at the Crown Inn at Dialpost, leave the car and explore the Knepp Castle area on foot; alternatively, on the walk past the grounds you will end up at the Countryman in Shipley, firmly in Belloc country. The church in Shipley also has some Norman features intact.

The Normans didn't just build castles on river and rape edges and deep upriver. They also constructed a small defensive site at **9. Castle Ring, Edburton Hill** north of Shoreham. This is one of the chain of Norman garrison posts that were built across the Downs. They were presumably built soon after the invasion, so that any invaders following the route one historian says they took westwards along the Downs as they explored Sussex, would be detected. Edburton Hill was also presumably an important lookout or signalling post for the Normans as the first site east of the Adur, so the first defence for invasion west towards Bramber Castle if any invaders copied the Romans and landed an invasion fleet in Chichester. It is technically located on the Fulking Escarpment but thankfully takes its name from the village of Edburton below as 'Fulking Fort' just sounds like someone grumbling about their sentry duty. Perhaps the sentries did grumble as it was probably an isolated fort, rather than a castle erected to suppress a local Park Brow-type settlement around it. However, the lost medieval village of Perching wasn't too far away from the castle, to the south-east. There is not much in the way of evidence and the low mutilated motte left just has some ditches and banks around what was a motte-and-bailey castle, with an unusual near-rectangular bailey. It can be easily missed without an OS map to identify the site. Castle Ring again takes a lot of imagination to envisage as a Norman site, but it is worth stopping at whilst you traverse the Downs on the way to or from Bramber Castle or Devil's Dyke, or during a visit to Norman Shoreham. It has been earmarked as a site of considerable archaeological potential, so perhaps this National Trust site may become a busy visitors' spot in the future. It needs to be reached on foot—the nearest car park is at Mill Hill, north of Shoreham.

Travelling south down the Adur to Shoreham we encounter a cluster of good Norman sites at Shoreham. As the Adur narrowed and silted up, St Cuthman's Harbour became less important and Old Shoreham developed. This is to the east of where the wonderful wooden toll bridge crosses the Adur today; unbelievably a one-car-wide roadway and part of the A27 until 1968. The Adur being much wider until the last millennium meant that this narrower section between Old Shoreham and where the Sussex Pad pub used to be (it's now part of Lancing College) provided a good route for a ferry crossing. A small harbour followed and development seems likely here since the Romans. It is believed a church existed on the site of the current **6. St Nicolas' Church** today since the 400s. By the 800s, a stone church existed and some of the Saxon stonework is still visible in the current church today. Its riverside location is remembered in the name of this settlement today, Shoreham meaning the farm or the homestead by the shore. Although St Nicolas could have been included in these earlier chapters, I have included it under the Normans not because it was first built then, but due to two reasons. Philip de Braose, son of William de Braose who took control of Bramber Rape decided to build New Shoreham further south due to the changing nature of the Adur, but this didn't mean St Nicolas' days were over. Philip built a new church, St Mary de Haura (of the harbour) in what would become known as New Shoreham, but he also ordered work on St Nicolas' Church, so it experienced a near-total Norman rebuild. The Saxon tower and several walls were demolished with transepts (the bits either side of the nave that make a church into a crucifix shape) and a new chancel (the bit where the vicar stands). St Nicolas also got a new tower and the church displays today a wonderful carved Norman doorway from this time. Craftsmen were probably brought over from

Normandy to build this church as it has a near-identical twin in Domfront, Briouze, from where William and Philip took their name. The other late Norman features that make the church unusual are carvings of the faces of King Stephen and Matilda. These are one of the few reminders in Sussex of this turbulent time (1135–1154) when the country was in rack and ruin as it suffered an ongoing civil war caused by the battles between these two to gain and keep the throne. Arundel was even besieged. Eventually a truce was reached that Stephen would rule whilst he was alive, but that Matilda's son, Henry II (as he became) would succeed him on Stephen's death. These effigies are quite fitting therefore for Old and New Shoreham, as New Shoreham would be the site of future development once Old Shoreham's day finished, just as Matilda's family would provide the future offspring of the English monarchy. The Norman era was over and the Angevins were poised to take over.

St Nicolas' Church, Old Shoreham, on the east bank of the Adur

Lunch Locally: Old Shoreham has two smashing old pubs—the Amsterdam Inn and the Red Lion. Both are overlooking the river and do food, with the Red Lion having the added bonus of having Tennyson written about it.

Sussex without Satnav: Walk back along the South downs Way to High Trees car park and drive through Upper Beeding to Bramber. From Edburton, drive back to the Shoreham Road, south to Upper Beeding and turn right at the Rising Sun pub, through Beeding and across the bridge to Bramber.

Old Shoreham Bridge

CHAPTER 5

Medieval Sussex

The Norman dynasty may have been replaced nationally as we move from the Norman era to the remainder of the medieval one, but the de Braose family would still remain supreme over Bramber Rape. Eventually the Norfolks of Arundel would inherit Lewes and take over Bramber—but by King John's time (1199–1216) the Braoses still were a powerful force to be reckoned with. John even told the de Braose family in 1208 he wanted two of the Lord's children as hostages to ensure their loyalty. William de Braose and his wife Matilda refused, as John was known to have murdered his young nephew Arthur, which incurred John's wrath and led to Matilda and her children being captured and thrown into John's dungeons to starve to death. William de Braose died of a broken heart. The ghosts of two of the children are said to still walk the road from the castle to Upper Beeding, begging for bread.

The de Braoses displayed their power and wealth in their building. St Andrew's Church at Steyning, which we have already discussed, has the 'chequerboard' pattern that was part of their coat of arms. The chequerboard was used for trade and commerce, and is why the oldest surviving pub in Steyning is called 'The Chequers'. The best example of the de Braoses ensuring this 'corporate' branding was seen across their land in Sussex (they had land down in Wales and Dorset too) was the building known as the **1. Marlipins Museum** today. This unusual two-storey building on Shoreham High Street is incredibly rare as we have few buildings from the early stages of the Middle Ages not with a religious or military purpose. It is believed to have been the customs house for this new port Philip de Braose built in the Norman era, but its facade was added it is believed later on in the fourteenth century. Its undercroft is where barrels of wine, port and brandy would have been kept. Shoreham became a very profitable port for three centuries and the front of the customs house was so designed to

Bramber Castle in the distance

remind people whose land this was and who charges would have to be paid to. This was nothing new for the de Braoses, as the first de Braose had built a bridge across the Adur so that people would pay to use his port there.

In the Middle Ages, **Bramber** and other castles including Chichester Castle would finally see action as they were captured in the little-known invasion of 1216 by Prince Louis of France against King John which was supported by many of John's barons. By this time John had seen off William de Braose, the latest in the de Braose line and his hunting lodge of **2. Knepp** had also been confiscated by that time by John, a king who no amount of revisionist work seems to rejuvenate the reputation of. John seemed to be fond of Knepp and several royal letters were written from there. He stayed there at least four times, before and after he seized it, in 1206, 1209, 1211 and lastly in 1214–5 when Queen Isabella was also in residence. By this time, it was a safer place for unpopular John, having been fortified in 1214 on John's orders.

Knepp was useful to John in other ways during his baronial wars and timber from the estate was used for helping defend Dover Castle, to unsuccessfully protect against his French invasion. Great moveable wooden engine-towers, (a cross between tanks and siege towers) were constructed from the woods of Knepp but to no avail, and by 1217 the country was largely under the control of the French prince, who very nearly became our first King Louis. It seems that felling of Knepp's trees became so comprehensive that John, (fearing a scene similar to that in Dr Seuss' *The Lorax*) ordered lumber to stop being cut. John's reign was thankfully instead cut back, due to him falling ill during his travels whilst Louis conquered swathes of his English land. By the end of his reign, John 'Lackland' (as he was known) had lost not only most of his lands overseas but his land in England too. We might have completely lost Knepp too, had John's servants carried out his orders to destroy it. Thankfully royal orders are not always carried out. Even so, we cannot but wish to see what this once-magnificent Royal resident and king's favourite hunting lodge was like at its peak in 1214. The de Braoses got Knepp back from Henry III, but its fate was to be its walls used as material for building what is now the A24 and it was demolished in 1726. There is a weird irony in that Sussex castles caused the development of some of our roads, which would themselves be improved by material from these castles.

Although the main families were trusted with the control of the six rapes established by the Normans, by later on into the Middle Ages, control was also maintained by the gentry and the clergy in smaller castles.

Tote Copse Castle - Continued fear of invasion and rebellion meant that these still played the role of lookout posts by the time, and the very name of

3. Tote Copse Castle (or Totehal as it was earlier called in the Domesday Book) suggests it was a lookout post even then. By the time of King Stephen (1135–54) a flint keep existed on a motte, with moat, ditch, bailey and curtain walls later added. This was no minor defensive site; the keep alone being approximately 39ft². Decay must have been allowed, however, as during the Civil War in 1648 the castle apparently fell to its attackers without a fight. The (believed to be adjacent) Aldingbourne manor house, also fortified in 1447 in the reign of Henry VI, was sold that year but oral tradition has it that the castle was in ruins by the time of the sale. In the 1960s the site was excavated as agricultural development was due, but caused damage to the remains. All that remains today is a flattened motte but the copse of trees indicate where the once-mighty motte and its keep once was, keeping watch proudly over this part of Sussex. There is another thirteenth-century motte castle at Lodsworth but it was so small and so little is left today there's nothing much to get excited about with this castle which protected part of Sussex's western River Rother.

Sussex without Satnav: We're looking at castles of the Middle Ages chronologically here, which leads to a spider's web of a route, so logically again you're best off starting in the west with Tote Copse first and then Barpham (which we mention shortly); the rest of the sites aren't too far apart from each other, but any route is a bit complex to be honest. Find the Fontwell roundabout on the A27 and head briefly south down the A29 to Nyton. Turn west towards Norton and take the next turn south to Westergate and you reach Tote.

Amberley Castle - Like Knepp, another one-time hunting lodge and inland castle is **4. Amberley Castle**, which also like Bodiam Castle was built due to concerns about the French. It was feared they would be able to increasingly attack the South by travelling far inland using Sussex rivers. Unlike Bodiam though, which was built by an individual, Amberley, like Tote Copse Castle, was fortified by the church to protect an existing archbishop's palace. The clergy needed protection just as the gentry did, due to their system of taxing too, with the system of tithe barns where the faithful would pay a tenth (tithe) of their crops or livestock. The late twelfth century halls of the ecclesiastical manor of Amberley are still intact within and were incorporated into later building work. Becoming a palace of the Bishops of Chichester was perhaps apt as it started life as a piece of land that was gifted to Bishop Wilfrid in 683 AD by Caedwalla, king of Wessex at that time. Another Bishop, Luffa, who also built Chichester Cathedral built a timber-framed hunting lodge in 1103 that was gradually transformed by the fourteenth century into a fortified manor house to protect Luffa's successors. By the time it was completed it boasted crenellations, battlements and a portcullis. It never saw any threats to its religious owners, but did suffer in the Civil War when Parliamentarians dismantled much of the castle in 1643 to stop it being a threat to their increasing military hold of the country. Sadly, the forces sent by General Waller destroyed 20–30ft of the curtain walls and even more sadly ruined the Great Hall. From being owned by men of the cloth, it was then sold to a cloth merchant, John Butler, who rebuilt the manor house from the Great Hall's ruins.

Amberley Castle

King Charles II can't have had much of a grudge against the former Roundhead stronghold though as he visited twice and it was returned to the Bishopric who leased it to Butler's family who stayed there for two more generations. The Church finally cut their ties with the building in 1872 when they sold it to Lord Zouche who owned Parham House. He continued to use it as a hunting lodge, just as Luffa had and then sold it to his more powerful neighbour, the Duke of Norfolk. The 15th Duke also used it as a hunting lodge, but repaired the portcullis and used it as his residence whilst Arundel Castle was under its substantial restoration programme. How nice to have your own backup castle! Since 1989 it has been a luxury hotel, owned by the Brownsword family, complete with a much-lauded restaurant, called the Queen's Room. This beautiful room has a barrel-vaulted ceiling, dating back to the twelfth century and along with the castle's history, views and location helps explain why it is a popular choice today for weddings.

Sussex without satnav: From Knepp, back down the A24 and then east along the A283 through Storrington, and head towards Arundel along the Houghton Road. Amberley Castle is reached just before you arrive at the Amberley Working Museum. It may be again that you explore Steyning, our next location and Knepp before heading down to Amberley as from Steyning there is a cut-through to Ashington and then up to Knepp before heading south to Amberley.

Lunch locally: Whilst in or near Amberley, you have of course the marvellous Bridge Inn, looking refreshed after a recent refurbishment or the Riverside Tea Rooms. Whilst we're featuring medieval Sussex though, the pub over the bridge and halfway up Houghton Hill is the George and Dragon, which dates back to 1276 and is one of the three oldest pubs in Sussex.

Sussex has several small medieval towns and villages where our medieval past is wedded to later buildings but still provides a hint of the middle ages; **Midhurst, Petworth and West Tarring** all have late medieval buildings, or buildings with some medieval portions. Tarring even has a row of fifteenth century cottages in its High Street.

Church Street, Steyning

5. Steyning, however, has not just buildings with medieval portions, but had a medieval port as well. It must be the town with the most comprehensive collection of buildings with medieval portions together though. It is even better than the Weald and Downland Living Museum, and with the added bonus of pubs and restaurants as you explore! Steyning was fortunate to be wealthy in the early Middle Ages so that its houses were substantial and well-built, but we are fortunate that its fortunes waned as its harbour silted up so that, unlike Lewes, there was less later wealth to rebuild the fronts of many of these buildings using later architectural styles. The town has not only legend and history on its doorstep, but is today the home of worldwide famous children's author Julia Donaldson, author of *The Gruffalo*. Julia Donaldson is a strong supporter of the wonderful independent Steyning Bookshop, so make sure you follow the example and buy some books there too! To tour Steyning on foot though, start at the opposite (Springwells) end of the town, walk north-west up the High Street as far as the Star pub, and then about-turn and take the left turn around the back of the High Street. You end at St Andrew's Church and the manor house, and then have the treat of Church Street to explore on your way back to the High Street, with its fine collection of buildings to feast your eyes upon. The High Street has one little treat in store for you that any visitor can enter as long as it's opening hours. The town's Post Office was built around 1360 and one of its beams inside has on view a Green Man carved into it, resplendent with vine leaves sprouting from his mouth and oak leaves shooting from his eyes. Theories as to why houses had these vary from tree worship to ritual protection for the buildings and those within them. Another is they were linked to the powers contained within your enemy's skull after killing them in battle. You too can ponder these possibilities as you queue up for a stamp, and the wonderful Post Office is also where you find the local tourist information point too.

Sussex without Satnav: A short trip, this one! Take the road out of Steyning past Springwells B & B and avoiding the road up the Downs to Steyning Bostal. At the Steyning/Bramber roundabout just past Steyning, take the third exit into Bramber village and our next destination is towards the bridge to Beeding on your right.

6. St Mary's House and Gardens - Parham, Danny, Streat in East Sussex and Wakehurst are all wonderful great houses, but St Mary's is built in the black and white late medieval style that so many 1930s banks and houses have tried to recreate. It looks like we imagine a house of this age should in Sussex, resplendent with its heavy Horsham slab roof. More amazingly, the house is the one remaining (east) wing of the original house, and all built on what was once only a causeway across the wide Adur Estuary. Like some other sites in Sussex, it has links with the mysterious Knights Templar, the land being given to them in 1125 by the widow of Philip de Braose, whom we mentioned earlier. The current building, built around 1470 by William of Wayneflete, Bishop of Winchester, became a monastic inn for travellers on the well-travelled route that was Beeding causeway who were heading for pilgrimage at Canterbury. William also repaired the bridge and was founder of Magdalen College, Oxford, suggesting he wasn't short of a pound or two like many bishops at this time. Nairn and Pevsner say on the site of the house was originally a chapter house, a home for the wardens of the bridge, who were monks from the nearby Sele Priory in Beeding. Its residents over the centuries have included MPs, farmers and even Charles II according to its owners, which seems unlikely as his escape over Beeding Bridge was one involving Parliamentarians in hot pursuit and his near capture. Beeding Bridge was once far wider (four spans) and its central pier was home to a small chapel of St Mary, from which the house eventually took its name. Its owners over the years have been inspired to maintain the house and have inspired both literature and even television. Its Victorian era owners, the Honourable Algernon Bourke, and his 'beautiful' wife Gwendoline, were most likely the inspiration for the characters in Oscar Wilde's famous play, *The Importance of Being Earnest*. Its Edwardian-era owner, Alfred Musgrave, was a wealthy socialite who was the inspiration for Arthur Conan Doyle's Sherlock Holmes book *The Musgrave Ritual*. St Mary's cellars also helped inspired Conan Doyle in writing the book apparently too. Described by Sir Simon Jenkins in his book *England's Thousand Best Houses* as 'a

Cowdray

shrine to medieval Sussex'. But St Mary's is much more than that, the changes to the building over the years tell a story of over five centuries.

From houses, towns and villages that have survived in part from the Middle Ages, to villages we lost, mostly due to the plague. Starting with the west of the county again, we start our explorations with the village of **7. Hooksway**. Hooksway and other local villages were decimated by the plague and never recovered, meaning the hard-to-find but worth finding Royal Oak (just off the Petersfield to Chichester road) is all that is left. Even walkers of the nearby South Downs Way have to make a decent detour to find this hidden inn, which until the 1970s had no electricity or even an inside toilet! There may not be anything left to see at Hooksway but any excuse to visit the Royal Oak and help support a remote Sussex pub must be a good thing. Thankfully it has toilets these days. In the seventies, the landlord Alfred Ainger was asked by the licensing authority about the sanitary arrangements, Mr Ainger replied, 'I have nine acres of field'.

Sussex without Satnav: Hooksway from Steyning is a bit of a jaunt. Take the A283 to Storrington, the B2139 to the A27 and then follow that until you pass Tangmere, where you head briefly up the A285 before heading north-westwards along the A286. Before you get to Binderton, take the B2141 past Chilgrove and you should reach Hooksway. Just past Storrington is Parham, which we mention shortly, so you should include that in your route first.

Changes in agriculture meant villagers deserted the village of **8. Barpham**, 3km to the east of neighbouring and similarly-named Burpham, which we mentioned under Saxon Sussex. The move to sheep-based agriculture meant fewer jobs existed and by the Black Death of 1348 finished the village off further, which was likely to be just to the west of Lower Barpham today. The manor house, like Parham, was seemingly separate from the villagers and is probably the site of Upper Barpham Farm today, sited higher up above the villagers in the valley and near the remains of the church, which was decommissioned finally in 1523 and can barely be seen. Barpham Church was probably ruined years even before that. Unlike Perching, though, Barpham does provide us with a vague outline of the layout of the houses, (as shown on the Geograph website) so you can walk around trying to picture the dying days of the village when bubonic plague finally finished off this Downland village which had existed since at least the eleventh century, and with its Saxon name, probably before.

Travelling eastwards again we arrive at **9. Parham** which had a village in the grounds of the great house today. The village was cleared by the owner of Parham, Sir Cecil Bishopp, the 7th Baronet (died 1779), who decided he wanted an uninterrupted view of the magnificent Downs to the south of the house and landscaped gardens. The pestilence-ridden village was cleared and the villagers redistributed south-westerly to the neighbouring village of Rackham, which still exists today and has the wonderful Sportsman pub nearby. Privacy was obviously the theme of the day if you had the money to buy it, as Parham House also diverted the road through the estate so ever since travellers from Storrington to Pulborough have to detour substantially.

Travelling westwards further, **10. Knepp**, which we have already mentioned, is believed to also have once had an attached medieval village. The basis of this belief stems from a 1754 map, that Richard Symonds of the Horsham District Archaeology Group has highlighted which shows an adjacent 'town field' next to the castle, usually signifying a lost medieval village, but further evidence is shown by King John ordering the houses to be destroyed at 'Knapp', and a later document also talks of its 'houses… all lands and tenements', as well as the way the fields by the castle were ploughed. With a north-south route nearby, the protection of a castle, good woodland for hunting and firewood as well as a large lake and river, this would have been a logical spot for a settlement. Similar inland castle sites such as Amberley, Bodiam and Bohun all generated or fostered settlements nearby so it seems logical Knepp could have done too.

11. Botolphs, south-east of Knepp by the Adur much nearer the coast is another deserted medieval village, but it grew up around the church there, which still exists today. Today a small rural settlement some distance from the Adur, in the early Middle Ages would have been riverside and earlier names for its church suggest that it was a busy bridging site for the Adur. It used to be called St Peter at the Old Bridge until the thirteenth or fourteenth century, the old bridge in question being left to neglect after the eleventh century construction of Bramber bridge. The double whammy of the semi-silting up of the Adur and the Black Death mean that today this Grade I church is a lonely survivor and reminder of what was once a thriving village, with only a few more recent houses keeping it company.

Sussex without satnav: From Knepp, come down the A24 and again back along the A283 when you pass Washington towards Steyning. Bypass Steyning and come to the roundabout with Bramber Castle's entrance on it. You need to turn south east down Maudlin Lane, down a narrow lane which is single-track in places and left onto the road south to Lancing College.

12. Perching (next to Edburton on the north-west slope of the Downs) further to the east was also probably a victim to the Black Death. Little exists above surface of this lost medieval village, and visitors today will be able to spot a Perching manor house, which is confusingly across the road from where the now-lost medieval manor house was. That house must have been substantial as the owners, the wealthy and influential Aguillon family, gained permission to crenellate the house at the time of the nearby Battle of Lewes, suggesting they supported the king at that time. They were lords of the manor for the majority of the 1200s and had acquired the territory which had been given to William the Conqueror's cook after the invasion. The house would have been to the east of where Perchinghill Barn is today and all that is visible are the slight remains of a moat. This was able to be filled as like the nearby Shepherd and Dog pub at Fulking, water emerged from the Downs at this spot, so much that there was even once a watermill and millpond. Despite the crenellated house, good income from the estate and water supply, the house and estate fell into ruin but we don't know why, nonetheless, not until the seventeenth century at least it seems. Perching Manor was further fortified in the 1300s and passed between several owners until the Civil Wars of the 1640s when its owner, another Royalist called Thomas Colstock, had to petition a committee to retain his property despite his loyalties.

Sussex without satnav: Back up Annington Road to the Bramber Castle roundabout and take the A283 eastern exit to Upper Beeding, north up to the Rising Sun and right along the A2037 until you get the Edburton Road on your right. Follow the Edburton Road until you pass Edburton—the new dwellings of Perching are on your left and the older settlement was on the right.

Medieval Churches

The majority of Sussex churches are Norman, with some Saxon remains if we are lucky and enlargements, rebuilding and improvements in the Middle Ages. Trying to find churches built solely in the medieval era after the Norman dynasty is trickier than it seems, but here I've just attempted to provide a taster of our medieval heritage. As we move further into the last millennium, Sussex has more and more choice in buildings to select and so here I've provided just some prime cuts. Moving westerly across the county therefore again, it is great to start with a medieval church with not just medieval scenes adorning its walls, but a rare Sussex link to the later Tudor era of Shakespeare.

13. St George Church (not St George's) in Trotton not only has marvellous brasses (something church enthusiasts get very excited about apparently) and scenes of medieval worship, sinning, repentance and biblical scenes all amazingly well-preserved in medieval technicolour. The brasses commemorate the local landowning de Camoys family, who were preserved for all eternity not just in brass and in their fourteenth-century tomb within the church, but by none other than the Bard.

Henry V must be one of Shakespeare's most famous and certainly most quotable of his plays, and Sir Thomas de Camoys was at the real Battle of Agincourt the play features. He was Henry's right-hand man, quite literally at Agincourt as he commanded the left flank of Henry's outnumbered and victorious forces. For his role in leading the troops to victory Henry awarded him the Order of the Garter and went on to enjoy a successful and lengthy career in Henry's diplomatic corps. Lady Elizabeth Camoys, who is buried next to him, was not only linked to Shakespeare, she was mentioned by him in an earlier play, *Henry IV*, where in her earlier marriage to Shakespeare's Henry Hotspur she is referred to as 'gentle Kate', despite being called Elizabeth. She was also granddaughter of Edward III. Part of the Latin text written on the Camoys brass reads: 'Pray for the soul of Thomas Camoys, and of Elizabeth his wife, who was once Lord of Camoys, baron and provident councillor of the King and Kingdom of England and zealous Knight of the Garter.' Thanks, we shall! Rarely for medieval women, we can see what Lady, another de Camoys, Margaret de Camoys looked like, as she is recreated in full-scale in a third brass. This is the earliest example in the whole country of a depiction of a woman in the whole of England, dating back to 1310. The de Camoys were a military family even then as Margaret's husband was at the Battle of Bannockburn against Scotland, where he was captured in 1315. You too will be not only captured, but entranced and delighted by this magnificent West Sussex church that tells us so much about nearly 300 years of our medieval and early modern past. Trotton was also the site of a particularly grizzly death in the Smuggling era of the 1740s, where Daniel Chater was tortured, thrown down the village well and stoned to death so he couldn't testify against a local smuggling gang.

Sussex without Satnav: The route from Edburton is the usual Steyning/ Storrington one but keep on the A283 once you've travelled through Storrington and it takes you eventually onto the A272, on which you will reach Trotton.

Lunch Locally: Should you be completing a marathon trek of medieval sites using this book and are continuing from Perching, then you have another longish journey, which may mean you'll probably need food at some point. Around Trotton is a bit of a wilderness for pubs so it may be that you fill up when passing through Petworth or Midhurst, the latter of which has a range of choices for noshing in its High Street and the sublime Spread Eagle Hotel for a quieter and more genteel setting for eating. There's also a spa to burn off your calories in afterwards, and the building's oldest parts date from 1430 so you have a late-medieval place to eat too. The building was built on the site of an even older medieval building, so you definitely can feel in touch with the Middle Ages during your meal. Another alternative en route is the Horseguards Inn in Tillington.

Heading back easterly to Worthing once more, **14. St Andrew's Church in West Tarring** brings us deep into this ever-growing settlement which, with a population of over 104,000 is larger than some UK cities. This wasn't always the case, however, as Worthing was once a collection of villages and the two Domesday manors of Ordinges and Mordinges which became the site of the seaside resort of Worthing. Tarring (the West part of the name is only added to distinguish it from Tarring Neville in East Sussex) was older and more established than Worthing by the Middle Ages, the first record of its existence being King Aethelstan granting it to what is now Canterbury Cathedral. The links with Canterbury remained for several centuries, with the land owned by the Archbishops of Canterbury, including Thomas Becket; local legend tells of him visiting the village and being linked to the archbishop's palace in the village, although no evidence of either has ever come to light and the palace's far later construction making the story impossible. The influence of Canterbury most likely means that St Andrew's is far bigger than other local churches of this era, which it needed to be as the local churches and chapels fell into disrepair following the Civil Wars and worshippers travelled here.

Its most famous worshipper was MP, writer and historian John Selden from nearby Salvington. Selden is seen as the nation's top historian of his time, who moved the nation's understanding of the past on, so it is good you can drink in the John Selden pub in Salvington and see a memorial to him at St Andrew's in Tarring. However, you can't visit the ancient cottage he was born in unfortunately as it burnt down from an electrical fault in 1959. The churchyard was once the workplace of a less law-abiding Sussex man, local leader of smugglers William Cowerson. Cowerson was a stonemason who is said to have hidden some of his contraband in the tombs he worked on in Tarring's church graveyard. On 21 February 1832, he used the church spire to signal to an approaching delivery that his gang of smugglers would intercept the beach landing that night. Cowerson was the leader of such a large smuggling gang that revenue officers in the area could only watch as goods were landed by 1832, protected by numerous staffmen, ruffians whose prime job description was to dish out concussion to any king's man who dared to intervene. The smugglers had clearly got too cocky after other successful landings and the customs men signalled for backup, which swiftly came. The gang scattered as they used the twittens of Worthing to escape. Worthing folk who lived in wealthy Warwick Street were even said to have let the smugglers in through their front doors and out the back, so confusing the revenue men giving chase and showing not only the poor of the county had interest in the low-priced smuggled goods. The gang ended up at the gate over the Teville Stream, at the top of what is now the High Street, which the town commissioners of the town had locked to keep vagabonds and other undesirables out. It now had the opposite effect and the smugglers could only escape to Findon or Broadwater one at a time.

Cowerson used his famously large frame (which was demonstrated by the size of his coffin) to block the small bridge to the gate whilst his men escaped. One of the leading revenue men, Lieutenant Henderson, had his arm broken by Cowerson, but still managed to fire at the smuggler at point-blank range, killing him. Cowerson's funeral and burial in Steyning was attended by over 1,000 people and their booty was never recovered by the revenue forces. Some believe that some of the stolen goods may still be hidden in the tombs at St Andrew's Church, which partly shares the name of the church where his grave can still be seen today. Those who believe in the supernatural may want to see which of the two St Andrews Cowerson would haunt—the one he was buried at or the medieval one in Worthing he would have worked on as a stonemason?

The Church of St Andrew and St Cuthman, Steyning, site of William Cowerson's grave

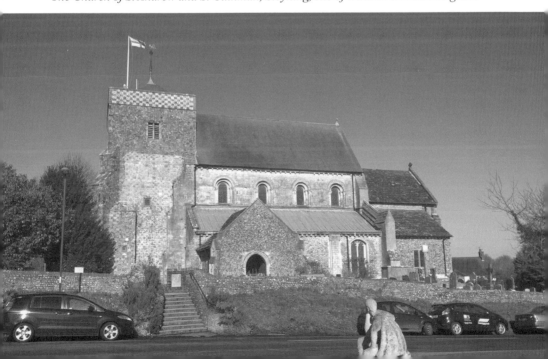

Finally, before we leave the Middle Ages firmly behind as the Tudors take over, we have one more site of note. **Lordington House**, today a bed and breakfast at the far west of the county and north-west of Funtington, was the home of Cardinal Pole, the last Catholic Archbishop of Canterbury. According to S.P.B. Mais' *Sussex in the 1930s,* it is haunted by his mother who was the last of the Plantagenets. She is still seen, according to the book, haunting the house with her throat cut, after her execution ordered when she was in her seventies by Henry VIII. This seems strange according to contemporary reports that her youthful executioner botched the job severely, leaving her head hacked to pieces and her neck not just severed but mutilated.

CHAPTER 6

Tudor & 'Second Iron Age' Sussex

The Tudor era is worthy of our time as it is the first time since the Romans with their Saxon Shore forts and to some extent Alfred the Great's burgs that there was ever an attempt to fortify the whole of the South coast. Henry VIII in the middle of the sixteenth century feared the combined wrath of France and Spain following the Reformation and so decided upon a chain of defensive works. Unfortunately for visitors to Tudor West Sussex only one was built at Camber, so we do not feature any in this publication, but this does mean that Sussex faced burnings and attacks in this era. Sussex also had a chain of warning beacons along the coast and across the Downs at the time of the Armada, part of the chain of beacons that covered the south and east of England. West Sussex's coastal ones were at West Wittering, Bracklesham, Selsey, Sidlesham, The Trundle, Pagham, Felpham, Littlehampton, East Preston, Kingston, Ferring, Goring, Heene, East Worthing, and Lancing. Some of the hilltop warning sites even gave us names of our most loved Downland peaks, such as Firle and Ditchling Beacon, but they were also on Highdown Hill, and Chanctonbury. There was also an Armada lookout post at Church Norton in Pagham Harbour that we mentioned in the chapter on the Normans. There are modern recreations of these beacons in several sites today. West Wittering's is the most picturesque but Worthing's, although in the wrong place being placed just west of the pier, reminds us that an ordinance survey undertaken in Queen Elizabeth's time of 'Worthing Shops' for potential defences is one of the first mentions of Worthing on record. Ordinance Survey is the name we use for the nation's official map firm today, but it means a survey of defensive potential, which is what occurred here. This survey is also the earliest appearance Worthing makes on a map.

North of Chichester, Midhurst is a tale not of two cities, but of two buildings, one destroyed and one surviving; the former, however, is nothing to do with Tudor warmongering. **1. Cowdray** would be one of England's finest houses if it hadn't caught fire in the 1700s. **2. The Spread Eagle,** however, has grown and prospered, as Cowdray withered. From its origins as one of the town's earliest inns, it has become one of the country's loveliest hotels today. It is West Sussex's version of the Mermaid Hotel in Rye.

Cowdray was a Tudor palace. Indeed, Charles Thomas-Stanford, one-time Mayor of Brighton, once described it as 'an almost royal state'. It was built to replace an earlier building, probably on the site built by the local de Bohun family, which in turn was to replace the nearby short-lived Bohunt Castle, which we mentioned earlier, sometime between 1273 and 1284. It has the rarity of being visited by both Henry VIII (three times), his son Edward VI and his youngest daughter, Elizabeth I, in 1591. Elizabeth is also said to have visited the Spread Eagle, to watch the festivities taking place in the town square below. Cowdray was built for comfort by Sir David Owen in the 1490s, who was Henry VIII's great-uncle, two reasons why it was popular with the Tudor monarchs, who would have appreciated the size and grandeur of this palace, said to be larger than anything else similar nearby. This grandeur can be explained by the fact it took sixty years to build, but still unfortunately just one day and night to burn down in 1793. Popular legend is that this was due to the Browne family, who inherited the house and Battle Abbey incurred the wrath of Battle Abbey monks they turfed out and one cursed the family, promising death by fire and water. It took over 200 years, but the long-term curse sounded eerily accurate when the house burnt down, the heir to the house drowned and the last in the line died childless. The house was also unlucky for Lady Margaret Pole, last of the Plantagenet line, for whom it was her last place of imprisonment before death in the Tower of London, and for Guy Fawkes who worked as a footman at Cowdray before his grisly end of torture and execution, the curse of death 'by fire and water, thy line shall come to an end' sounding familiar here too. Had the 2nd Viscount Montague (as the Brownes were known) stayed away from Parliament after the warning that Parliament was due to be attacked by Fawkes and the other plotters, then Parliament might have looked in 1605 as Cowdray does today. The curse seemed to pass onto the Poyntz family who married into the Browne family, as both their sons drowned in 1815. Not until

Cowdray

the 1880s was a replacement house built for the surviving branch of the family, and that was elsewhere in Cowdray Park. By that time, the ruins were crumbling, aided by ivy growing all over the walls. An earlier attack on Cowdray's walls was by musket balls, still visible today, from when the estate was a Roundhead soldiers' garrison, taken from the Catholic-supporting Montagues during the Civil War. It is indeed surprising the house didn't burn down in the 1640s then instead with anti-Montague troops at large.

The one surviving part of Cowdray that didn't burn down from the 'Cowdray Curse' was the kitchen tower, which can still be seen today. This is where Britain's top chef of the 1600s, Robert May, was employed. Not only the top chef for a leading aristocratic family, May also wrote one of the country's earliest cookbooks thirty years later, *The Accomplisht* [sic] *Cook*, which sounds as if the chef had had one too many cooking sherries when he was writing the title.

Excellent cuisine can still be found in Midhurst today, but more likely at the Spread Eagle, five minutes' walk from Cowdray. Cowdray was famously little changed from its Tudor beginnings until its fire in 1793, which is why Samuel Johnson famously said of Cowdray that he would like to stay there for twenty-four hours, as 'we see here how our ancestors lived'. The Spread Eagle has maintained its early, late-medieval sections, but unlike Cowdray has expanded, adding sections under its spread eagle's wing from the centuries since to provide a journey through time for those who stay there. Those who journey to Midhurst's oldest hotel not only get to stay in a timber-framed structure with a jettied front that is partially built of wattle and daub, but other wings from other centuries. They also experience the place where Lord Nelson visited. Nelson's mistress Emma Hamilton was the wife of Sir William Hamilton, MP for Midhurst between 1761–74. Nelson visited later than this time though, at some point between 1791–8. Another famous ladies' man was King Edward VII, who seems to have been particularly fond of Sussex going by his numerous visits over the years. Edward had a German surname, thanks to his father being Prince Albert so, of course, did Hermann Goering and Hitler's Ambassador to Britain, Von Ribbentrop, who stayed in July 1939, only two months before the outbreak of the Second World War. Perhaps seeing the similarity of the hotel's eagle signs to the Nazi eagle as a lucky omen the thirties, version of the Chucklebrothers visited Goodwood to watch the horseraces there, before dining at the hotel. Following the war, the hotel attracted thankfully visitors who weren't planning invasion, such as David Bellamy, Roger Whittaker, Trevor Howard, Prince Charles and Sir Cliff Richard.

My favourite time to visit the Spread Eagle is in the winter when you can relax in its cosy lounge bar with a roaring log fire. Also, should you stay over the Christmas period, you will witness a culinary tradition with a difference. Residents who stay for Christmas and want to return the following year must all hang a Christmas pudding from the ancient oak beams in the seventeenth century dining room. Hilaire Belloc wrote 'The Spread Eagle of Midhurst, that oldest and most revered of all the prime inns of this world.' There is very little that can be added to that, so I won't, and we will move south-east and back down towards the A27.

Sussex without Satnav: Take the A285 south until you're on the outskirts of Chichester. Take the first left onto New Road, which then takes you onto the A286 in a north-easterly direction to Halnaker.

3. Halnaker House was rebuilt soon after 1525 and is located a mile north of Boxgrove, by the 9th Baron De La Warr from whose family the name of Delaware, USA originates. The family's achievements don't stop there, however, with inspiring names of US places, but include fighting for Henry V at Agincourt in 1415, the wrong side in the Wars of the Roses but then for Henry VII to suppress a Cornish uprising led by the pretender to the throne, Perkin Warbeck. The 9th Baron did his best to impress alongside Henry VIII at the Field of the Cloth of Gold, the Tudor Anglo-French peaceful coexhibition of friendly rivalry and one-upmanship in 1520. We feature it under the Tudors as nine years later the king would be entertained at Halnaker, which is in itself an achievement as a rare fortified Sussex manor house. Amberley is more of a castle than fortified manor so having a house that once had its own curtain wall, not to mention bear pit, is indeed a find. Halnaker never saw any action and so it was time and ruination that were to be its greatest enemies, not action of any type. If all of this doesn't tempt you to visit then it is likely that the original twelfth century house, built by Roger de Haye, is probably under the current buildings, which were also rebuilt in the fourteenth century and weren't allowed to fall into ruin until the 1880s. De La Warr also faced a ruinous decision eventually—he fell out with Henry over the dissolution of the monasteries and the king told him he was to swap Halnaker (which he'd rather taken a fancy to) for Wherwell Abbey in Hampshire. The choice was either nuns or none, and the Baron went for the former. It is quite ironic that the man who protested over the king's dissolution of the monasteries ended up with one. Thankfully for them, the family still had another property at Offington in Worthing, to dissipate their hardship. Halnaker ended up as the property of the Dukes of Richmond, who neglected it in the 1800s when they were developing Goodwood and we are left today with a romantic and thought-provoking ruin.

Sussex without satnav / Lunch Locally: We're travelling next down what should be a familiar route by now easterly along the A27 to Fontwell, the A29 until the roundabout north of Arundel. There is an interesting cafe in the car park here, which can get busy when throngs of motorbikers descend upon it. Take the B1239 down through Houghton and Amberley, but turn left at the next left after Rackham Street and it takes you on a very charming little route right practically to the entrance to Parham—just

Above: *Parham House*

Below: *Wiston House*

turn left. On the way from Halnaker you have the George and Dragon at Houghton with amazing views to the rear, a choice of the Bridge pub in Amberley, or the tea room and the Sportsman at Rackham is not too far off your route. The nearest pub to Parham is the Crown Inn at Cootham which has a good garden for young ones.

4. Parham, Danny and Wiston House are all magnificent examples of trophy Tudor houses at their finest, but as Wiston is only rarely available to the public for tours and events, and Danny is a residential retirement home with only rare opportunities for tours we feature only Parham here. It is here, just to the west of Storrington, that a hall existed, possibly on the same site as the earlier and existing Tudor house today. It was once believed that some of the earlier house had been incorporated into the current building, but that theory has since been disproven. The current house was built on land that had been owned by Westminster Abbey before the Tudor era, but it was in the time of Henry VIII that the story of Parham (pronounced Parr-ram as in 'parrot', not Pah-ram) really begins.

The dissolution of the monasteries and the sale of church land under Henry VIII in the Reformation gave Henry's loyal supporters, such as Robert

Parham

Palmer a mercer of London, the opportunity to gain grants to religious estates and move up the social ladder. The fairly elderly Palmer gained the earlier Tudor grange that was on the current site of Parham Park today to add to his property portfolio, but as the family were mostly based in Somerset they didn't spend that much time there. Later generations of Palmers didn't either, but it would be Robert Palmer's great-grandson Thomas who laid the foundation stone for a new house in 1577 at the age of two and a half (it's whereabouts is missing today, sadly). Foundation stones belonging to the Palmers were not the only thing in the 1500s being laid into the soil, great-grandpa Palmer was also buried in Parham Church according to his will, along with a memorial which has disappeared over the years. What has also disappeared is the accompanying village that was near to Parham House, matched by the removing of the villagers to nearby Rackham. Despite the village being in existence as relatively recently as the 1770s, we have no exact idea where it was. Perhaps *Time Team* will one day come back on our screens and pay a visit to solve the mystery? It is suspected that it was by the Church though; local archaeologists think looking at pathways and comparing with other medieval villages. A building older than Parham House has been discovered but not much else. Parham is unusual in facing south where the village was once in view; most stately homes faced away from where they thought miasma (unhealthy air) would pass across the channel from the 'filthy French'.

Young Thomas' stone-laying set him in good stead for a memorable life and this ritual, which was meant to be good fortune for a house, seems to have saved it from Cowdray-like curses so the house we see built around that stone is still the one we see today, four and a half centuries later. The boy who laid that stone went on to become an adventurer with Sir Francis Drake and became Sir Thomas Palmer, being knighted for his role in the seizing of Cadiz in 1596. He died in 1605, four years after selling the house to what would be only the second family to own Parham, the Bishopps. The Palmers were still the family that owned the house when it is believed Queen Elizabeth visited. Bess' god-daughter, Elizabeth Verney, lived at Parham so it is likely she would have popped in en route to Cowdray in 1591. Elizabeth's coat of arms hangs in the Great Hall and states '*Semper eadem*'—'always the same' in Latin, but it has not always been the same. Originally it stated '1583' the year the house was believed to have been completed, but Victorian workmen restoring the panel changed it to the date it shows now, with the 8 substituted somehow for a 9. Changing dates are not the only thing that move at Parham—a portrait of Charles I cleverly has a foot that follows your gaze as you move left past the painting!

The Bishopps' ownership of Parham started with Thomas Bishopp of Henfield who was a local MP; it was subsequently owned by five consecutive Sir Cecil Bishopps. The 8th Baronet, who became Lord Zouche, was also responsible for the building of the southerly Storrington to Houghton turnpike road, which he did jointly with the Duke of Norfolk. Mary, the seventeenth Baroness Zouche, would go on to sell the house to Clive and Alicia Pearson, (who were the children of the owners of Cowdray) in 1922. During the Second World War, the Pearsons took in thirty evacuees from Peckham, many of whom maintained links with Parham for decades afterwards. In 1942, Canadian Infantry soldiers responsible for the defence of Sussex's coast moved in, but thankfully the divisions included engineers who could fix any damages they made, so unlike other requisitioned houses, such as Castle Goring, Parham saw the end of the war in a relatively good condition.

Parham, due to continued investment since the 1920s, is in an even better condition today. According to Sir Simon Jenkins in his *England's One Thousand Best Houses*, Parham is in his top twenty. He goes on to say, 'Nothing at Parham is superfluous, nothing unloved. It is a house of magic.' This has been largely as the Right Hon Clive Pearson and his wife Alicia, who bought the house and grounds in 1922, had by 1948 sensitively, caringly and diligently repaired the ageing house. You can still feel today the pride the Pearsons must have felt in the restoration of what is truly a gem of Sussex and one of the nation's finest Elizabethan houses. Clive and Alicia Pearson's descendants, Lady Emma Barnard and her family, evidently still have the same pride today and the house and its grounds provide not just a window to the past but a number of mysteries.

The Tudor era was not just about overseas expansion and posturing with trophy houses, it was about industry too and an early equivalent of the Industrial Revolution took place in Sussex, with iron being big business. You wouldn't think it when you tour the Weald today, but Sussex's greenest area was once its most industrial. Sussex place names such as Hammerpot, Furnace Green and anywhere with 'hammer' in the name remind us that the county helped defeat the Armada with the cannon being forged in our furnaces. Elizabeth Palmer (née Verney) of Parham in the Great Hall of the house, has cannon embroidered over her dress to perhaps suggest the industrial might Sussex had at this time. Likewise, one of our prettiest areas we have already visited in the Tudor era and seventeenth century was one of our most industrial. **5. Knepp Mill Pond** in the grounds of Knepp Castle is man-made and was at one point the biggest body of inland water in Sussex. It once supplied water to not just one but two iron mills at Knepp to help make metal. Before coal took over, the plentiful supply of Sussex Wealden trees kept the iron furnaces going and Sussex's streams and rivers helped provide the water needed for cooling and smelting and a head of moving water to turn waterwheels to power hammers to crush iron ore or power bellows to work a furnace.

There is debate over when the pond was created from the much-tamed Adur at this point, which once also helped protect the nearby castle. The iron furnace and forge at Knepp, to the south-east of Knepp Pond, belonged to the Duke of Norfolk and was run for him by the Caryll family, who ran it from 1568 to 1604 when it stopped production. A reminder today of this is Furnace Lodge, which is on the A24 nearby. The pond could have been created by building a dam at least before 1326, as there is record of a watermill in Knepp even then. The owner of Knepp Castle Sir William Burrell in 1780 put forward the theory that the castle and land took its name from a flat pond, with 'Knepp' coming from the French phrase '*Nape d'eau*', meaning 'sheet of water in the form of a table cloth'. This could suggest the pond was in existence before the castle's eleventh century construction. This would mean it could be the site of very early ironworks indeed. A nearby furnace at Shipley which shared the local waters was still working by 1641, when the Sussex iron industry enjoyed a brief boom in creating weapons for the Civil War (there were still about twenty-seven furnaces at that time), but increasingly cheaper Swedish imports by the late 1600s and by the Scots in the 1700s signed the death warrant of the industry. Sussex's last ironworks finally closed in 1827. Today, you couldn't imagine a less-industrial location, with the pond's tranquil and almost-still waters, its haven for wildlife and views of distant Downland. Yet with some imagination you can hear the pounding of hammers, the roar of the furnace and the hiss of the waters at Knepp cooling iron products several centuries back.

6. Wakehurst, our final stop in our travels across Tudor Sussex is a three-for-one visit. Not only do you get one of the prettiest Elizabethan houses in the country, built in 1590, you also get the world's largest seed conservation project and a huge botanical garden. It is also where the National Trust and the Royal Botanical Gardens of Kew come together, as the National Trust owns the site which Kew uses for its Millennium Seed Bank project. Like St Mary's House in Bramber, it was originally built around a courtyard, but now only one wing exists, so it copies the traditional 'E' shape we expect from Elizabethan houses. Wakehurst Place Mansion was itself copied by the Americans in 1887 so a replica today exists in Newport, Rhode Island and is today owned by the Salve Regina University. Aptly for a Tudor building, it was used by Kenneth Branagh in his 2006 film of *As You Like It*. Shakespeare's *Twelfth Night* has never been filmed there but is the date until which the country's largest growing Christmas tree is lit every year with around 1,800 lights at Wakehurst from the start of Advent. This is just one of the things that makes Wakehurst usually the National Trust's most popular property. Should a complete Elizabethan property be too much for you to take, then ration yourself with a visit to nearby Slaugham Place in Haywards Heath, whose ruins today are the remainder of the last large house built in Sussex in the Elizabethan era and used for weddings today. Should you choose to put a bit of valuable metal around your finger and get married there, then it is most apt as, like Wiston, the family that built it made their money from the 'New Iron Age' in Sussex.

Sussex without Satnav: Despite crossing mid-Sussex, this is a simple journey that involves mostly that quintessentially Sussexian road, the A272, which has even inspired its own book. Follow the A272 until the B2036 in Cuckfield. Take Hanlye Lane, Copyhold Lane, College Road and then finally the B2028 to Wakehurst Place.

Lunch Locally: Not exactly 'locally' this time, as none of our Tudor buildings mentioned above are near it, but the Kings Head in Upper Beeding dates back from 1504 and the Chequers or the Norfolk Arms in Steyning both date back to Tudor times.

CHAPTER 7

Stuart, Civil War and Restoration Sussex

The relative stability of the Tudor era and its boom in building of houses was swapped for the instability, division and intermittent civil wars that were the legacy of the Stuarts. A more inept, treacherous and costly royal dynasty is hard to find, and before long into the first Stuart's reign, Jacobean housebuilding swiftly turned into great house and castle destruction by the actions during what still remains England's costliest war per capita. The only houses of distinction are Great Ote Hall, rebuilt in 1600, and Albourne Place built in 1650 just after the wars finished (more about there later) in West Sussex. It is to the Restoration and the later Stuart era we need to look for amazing places to visit, such as Petworth House and Uppark.

Sussex's Civil War action happened mostly early in the wars of 1642–49 and is unusual in that it occurs in the winter. Most Civil War action was in the summer, as it was the best time for campaigning with muddy roads dried and passable. These Sussex winter actions only happened as an unusually hard frost that winter made the roads manageable, but it means most of the few Sussex sieges and battles occurred with a frozen and frosty backdrop. Those who fell to the pike or the musket on the streets or fields of Sussex would have laid shivering as their lifeblood ebbed out of them. Sussex action was rare as the county was not only hard to traverse but also mostly woody still at this stage. Our action in West Sussex therefore takes place in towns, clearings such as Muster Green and unusually, on a bridge. Sussex's geographical location took it away from most of the fighting nationwide, and the pro-Parliament leanings of its inhabitants meant that it tended to be Royalist areas such as Chichester in the far west that really needed incursions from what would become Cromwell's forces. Sussex was probably more useful to Parliament in terms of its 27-odd furnaces for making munitions and being a gateway to guard against Royalist imports from the Continent. Talking of imports, the Roundhead monopoly of Sussex meant Charles needed to bring in his ordinance from the West Country, helping explain Royalist supremacy nearer that half of the country. We see early Civil War action in Sussex, except for at Arundel, some last-minute drama as the war reignited in 1648–9, but apart from that we provided munitions, not memorable battles, and our soldiers were drafted to help elsewhere, such as the dramatic siege at Old Basing House in Hampshire.

Sussex Civil War action is mostly about sieges, so we should commence our exploration of Stuart and Civil War Sussex with a decent pub first, as for the true experience of Civil War siege conditions you should afterwards avoid food to recreate the hardship soldiers in Arundel Castle faced during its lengthy second siege. Should you want to prepare yourself to recreate the siege Cicestrians would have faced, then just have a light lunch as the siege was not a long one, only lasting for five days. The earliest Civil War action of 1642 isn't at Chichester, but it is that end of the county again we start so lunch locally at the **1. Crab & Lobster in Sidlesham**, as it also featured in the Civil War. The pub and area are still said to be haunted by a local Royalist commander, Sir Robert Earnley or, if not at least him, one of his men. The man was reported to have been shot dead by Roundheads on the harbour's edge and dragged a mile or so to the former pub that existed here in Mill Lane before the current one. Pagham Harbour was being used as a staging post for Cavaliers attempting to flee the advancing Roundheads in the 1640s. The nearby hamlet of Earnley shares its name from his family who were lords of the manor dating back to the Middle Ages and they too shared their surname with one of the senior Civil War Commanders.

As a Royalist, Earnley faced what seems to be a gruesome death for choosing what would become the losing side and the opposite team to most of Sussex, which was generally on Parliament's side during the war. It was only the leading families that seemed to stay loyal to King Charles, and so they sometimes forfeited their land, or just kept their heads down for the duration.

2. Chichester being a walled city meant that Parliament, under Sir William Waller, needed to control it as part of his control of the South. 'William the conqueror' as he became known, needed to besiege the garrison town as the Parliamentary forces within had been driven out by August 1642 and Royalist Sir John Morley was firmly in charge, supported by the High Sheriff of Sussex, Sir Edward Ford. Ford was a ruthless leader, forcing locals to enlist to protect Chichester and join him on threat of having their houses burnt if they didn't. Waller had a battle on his hands when he arrived on 21 December 1642 as the Royalists originally advanced, but after being repulsed by the Roundheads the medieval walls of the city made a defensive strategy the best bet, so a siege commenced as the Royalists took up defensive positions behind the walls.

To explore the action of the siege best, start at the East Gate of the city. The parish there of St Pancras still has scenes of the bombardment on show, and the original church was mostly destroyed as a result of its Civil War role and not rebuilt until 1749, over a century later. This was because the church of St Pancras, which had been on the current site since the Middle Ages, was used to attack the city walls and gate, with cannon being hoisted up to the church tower to blast away at the recalcitrant Royalists late in December 1642. The technique eventually worked (along with attacks on the South and West Gates) and the city surrendered to Parliament's force of approximately 6,000 after five days without further bloodshed after soldiers broke through an old bricked up gateway. St Pancras had been a thriving industrial area for the city in the 1640s with locals making needles in their houses. This industry was lost, as many houses were destroyed by the soldiers within the garrison, firing fire to burn them to keep their attackers away, a tactic that worked at the West Gate of the city. It was apparently years before the houses in the St Pancras district were rebuilt and by that time those involved in the industry were dead or had fled elsewhere.

After exploring St Pancras, follow the route the Parliamentarians would have taken after they entered the city by following the predictably named East Street from East Gate westerly to the cathedral. Chichester is mostly pedestrianized in the centre, so best to park at the car park just outside of the East Gate, next to the small cinema. When you reach the cathedral try not to do what the Parliamentarians did and desecrate it, apparently watched on by the Roundhead leaders. Decorations were torn down, tables and the organ destroyed and even prayer cushions were ripped apart. Tombstone inscriptions were hacked with swords, paintings and decorations slashed. Thankfully the main fabric of the cathedral—walls, some windows and the like were left intact and the city wasn't plundered, unlike Winchester. The cathedral today is still intact, but nevertheless mentions the grander features and fittings that were destroyed. Anything that could be stolen from the cathedral was stolen but evidently this didn't satisfy Parliaments' desire for destruction as when the cathedral was despoiled as much as possible, the Roundheads then broke into a small church nearby and did the same again. In the carnage, the Protestant Edward VI's portrait had its eyes gouged out and one Frenchman had his wooden foot broken.

You may also wish to visit the South and West Gate areas of the city (still easily signposted and west and south of the easily-findable market cross) if you wish to see where Waller planned to simultaneously attack using petards on the sixth day of the siege if the Royalists hadn't surrendered. When the Royalists at Chichester surrendered, one Colonel George Gunter was captured. We shall meet him later, when he helps Charles II to escape to the Continent via Sussex.

The Parliamentarians would stay until 1646 at Chichester and the city was held as a garrison until then. Just before the heat of action in 1642 though, the Royalists who had been holding Chichester launched an advance before the siege to Lewes and their comrades-in-arms faced another attack at Arundel. We mention them now as we move eastwards once more. Chichester wasn't attacked by Waller's full force; about 100 of his men branched off with the orders of securing **3. Arundel Castle**. Sir Richard Rochford was the garrison commander there and obviously wasn't aware that being in a large castle made you a prime target for attack as his forces were unprepared for Waller's smaller forces attack that December. This makes for a bit of a mystery: why would the easily-defendable Arundel Castle have witnessed little preparation for attack, which could have made it near impenetrable, whereas Chichester in the flat lands north of the harbour, only defended by elderly medieval walls, was where the Royalists decided to keep the majority of their forces and make their bigger stand? Unlike in earlier days, it seems the Lavant no longer seemed to be usable as protection. Arundel could have been the site of a long and complicated siege, and a central source of resistance, in the centre

Arundel Castle

of a largely-Parliamentarian county. The answer may be religious; perhaps the Royalist leader Ford was ordered to defend Chichester Cathedral at any cost and its treasures from the ransacking and refinery-hating puritans in Parliament's forces, especially after the plundering of Winchester. Arundel was also missing its lord, its owner, Thomas Earl of Arundel had wisely removed himself to the Continent in 1641 and his son and heir was elsewhere fighting for the King.

Whatever the priorities of the Royalists, Arundel was soon taken and with no costs to Waller's forces—not one Roundhead soldier died in its capture. A petard, an early bomb, whose name interestingly partly comes from the French phrase 'to break wind' was used to destroy the castle gates and the measly hundred defenders were soon beaten by a force of only thirty-six men (the other sixty-four were being used to keep any Royalist townsfolk from helping the castle defenders, in case you wondered). Visitors today can still see some of the cannonball grooves from the short battle that took place at the castle in this siege, which was even more brief than the later Chichester one. One outcome was that Arundel would face a counter-attack the following year by the Royalist invasion into Sussex and all of this led to it being partly ruined for years. It wouldn't be restored properly until the Victorian era. Another consequence was the capture of 100 horses, arms and stores, which meant that even the most poverty-stricken foot soldier may have had a taste of what it was like to be one of their much wealthier opposition, whose nickname was 'Cavaliers'. The poorer Royalist prisoners-of-war faced a dangerous journey by sea to London for imprisonment there, whereas the wealthier Cavaliers were sent by road. Sir Edward Ford soon managed to worm his way back into the king's army and, like the army itself, was not beaten yet.

This wasn't the end of the story though for Arundel, as the Royalist leader Hopton invaded the county in yet another December operation on 5 December 1643 from the north-west. The Royalists were stronger in Kent and on the Hampshire border, and so joining up their forces in Sussex made strategic sense. Earlier houses on the sites of Uppark and Petworth to the west of the county (extreme west in Uppark's case) were both raided in this year, with Petworth's owner, the Lord of Northumberland, losing twenty of his best horses which ended up with Charles' forces in Oxford. Horse stealing seems a bit like the capturing of naval 'prizes' in the Napoleonic Wars or even the Germans nicking British tanks in the First World War—yours may well have started off as your enemy's.

Hopton arrived at Arundel on 6 December followed by Waller and local Parliamentary leader, Colonel Morley of Glynde, who recaptured Cowdray and reached Arundel nearly two weeks after Hopton. Arundel Castle had fallen to the Royalists after three days, but it would take over a year for Waller to oust the 1,000-strong garrison that Hopton had installed at the castle, despite Waller's 10,000-strong force. The eventual Royalist surrender would only be achieved with the cutting off of the castle's water supply from nearby Swanbourne Lake (a charming stream-side walk from the castle today) and the destruction of much of the town of Arundel. This destruction goes some of the way to explain why such an ancient town as Arundel today mostly dates from the late seventeenth, eighteenth and nineteenth centuries, but little from before. Apart from the Norman Keep and Barbican from the 1300s, the castle was destroyed, as was the Crown's hold on the county from that point.

Sussex without Satnav: From Chichester you simply need to follow the A27 east to Arundel. From there you can carry on to Lewes to see where the Royalists were trying to make their way to, or go straight to Haywards Heath via the A27, A23 and then east on the A272. See previous 'Lunch Locally' sections for information on places for food at Chichester—for Lewes recommendations, you'll have to wait for *Visitors' Historic Britain: East Sussex*!

Lunch locally: The Loft at Sparks' Yard in Arundel is heartily recommended for a good feed with good views across the town's rooftops and valley from the town. The Californian-themed cuisine means a burger to die for and a shop and coffee shop below to make your visit a worthwhile experience. Alternatively, Arundel has many fine pubs, and should you want to get as close as you can to the castle's owners still today, then nosh at the Norfolk Hotel, next to the rebuilt castle.

Haywards Heath - Back to 1642 before Chichester and Arundel's first siege, Sir Edward Ford led an advance north and east towards Lewes but never made it that far. In December 1642 they were intercepted by the Roundheads at Muster Green, in what is now **4. Haywards Heath** today. It is believed that the spot was where the church is now but back in the 1640s this was open (and not yet Hayward's) Heath. This is West Sussex's only Civil War battlefield of any size in open land. Neither side had any artillery, and it was the Royalists who took a pasting, with their advance routed and around 200 of their soldiers dead or injured in an hour. Ford's men either scattered or returned with him to Chichester where the final major Civil War action, the siege of Chichester, was yet to come. Philip Pavey, author of *Mysteries of History In Sussex*, claims that had the Royalists won, the outcome could have been decisive, but there is little evidence that one relatively insignificant battle in what was a Roundhead-controlled region could have given Charles' forces the impetus they needed to halt the losses of 1644 and 1645.

Lunch Locally: There is only one choice if you want to eat near Muster Green. Formerly known as The Dolphin, The Sergison Arms is named after the Sergison family, who historically owned large areas of farmland in and around Haywards Heath. The building predates the Civil War battle as it was built in the sixteenth century; it is thought to be one of the oldest buildings in the town and began life as a private dwelling called Vynalls, named for John Vynall (d.1599).

Following this the county remained in Parliament's hands for the rest of 1642, with only a minor skirmish at the bridge at Bramber in 1642.

As mentioned, 1643 saw the start of the second siege of Arundel and some other small occurrences. At South Harting on 23 November 1643 there was a small fight, with three soldiers buried the following day as a result, and a further fight at Stansted Park (near the Hampshire border) in April 1644 led to the house, dating back to the Norman era, being destroyed. Today, St Paul's Chapel in the grounds of Stansted Park is where the ruins of the house were and was built in 1804.

Arundel, as mentioned, faced an attack with Parliamentarians experiencing, not leading the attack this time. Culminating in an uprising in 1648 at Horsham, Sussex seems to have been more annoyed with having to feed and accommodate troops of either side, but especially Parliament's. This resulted in meetings of the anti-war faction known as the Clubmen, after the home-made and improvised weapons many carried. This could be serious; two soldiers were murdered by villagers of Nuthurst near Horsham in 1644 and large meetings took place at Bury Hill, Duncton Down and Rooks Hill (the alternative name at that time for The Trundle that we featured earlier). At the last of these, over 1,000 locals attended and these meetings were seen as such a threat that Cromwell personally ordered their dispersal.

Before we return to the west of the county and follow the fugitive Prince Charles' route across the county to French freedom, we need to tell one last tale of adventure in the east of the county; somewhere that has even been East Sussex before 1974. From Haywards Heath, take the A272 back to the A23 and south to Albourne.

5. Albourne House had a history of supporting the monarchy, even to the extent back in the twelfth century when Sir Ranulph de Broc, the house's heir, was one of the four knights who misinterpreted Henry II's order and liberally smeared Thomas Becket's brains over Canterbury Cathedral's floor. Loyalty to royalty was still the order of the day five centuries later and the brother of Albourne Place's owner, William Juxon, the Bishop of London said prayers with Charles I as he awaited execution in 1648. Juxon was a man of cunning as well as of the cloth, and he is said to have escaped Roundhead forces hunting him following his support for Charles by pretending to be a bricklayer at his brother's house, which was undergoing building work. Not so much a man of God, but a man of hod (carrying). The Bishop looked busy whilst Parliament's forces searched the building site and his work must have been convincing as Parliament's soldiers didn't notice that the chimney he was working on was becoming unusually broad as he kept trying to look busy. Cromwell's men never captured him and after his services to the elder Charles, Juxon managed to enjoy a peaceful semi-exile in Gloucestershire during the Interregnum, before being appointed Archbishop of Canterbury by the younger Charles in 1660. It ended the Civil Wars being sold, ironically to a Parliamentarian and still stands today, but is now divided up into separate private houses, the oldest part of which is called Old Threel House and dates from the fifteenth century. It is amazing that here in Sussex we have the house owned by the brother of the last man to hear some of Charles I's last words.

Sussex without Satnav: From Haywards Heath to Albourne, the simplest if least direct route is the A272 westwards and then the A23 southwards until you get onto Mill Lane (the B2118). At Albourne, take the B2116 west until Truslers Hill Lane and head south here towards the Downs. Albourne Place is on your left but is a private house, so the nearest you can get is the Albourne Farm Estate Vineyard and Winery—which seems a civil place to toast those who were involved in the Civil War!

Lunch Locally: Albourne has the wonderful Ginger Fox a short drive away as well as fantastic family-owned coffee and farm Shop at Rushfields Garden Centre for great Sussex food and drink. These can be accompanied afterwards by a visit to Bedlam Brewery, run by Alison and Nick Nightingale—or you could just stock up for a local liquid lunch! Albourne has no pub of its own, but there is the nearby Duke of York on Sayers Common en route from Haywards Heath too.

The domination of the county by Parliament is what made Charles Stuart's (eventually Charles II from 1660–1685) Great Escape across West Sussex in the autumn of 1651 following defeat at the Battle of Worcester all the more remarkable. Charles followed the road in past Uppark to Arundel, up the Hill towards Bury and then down through Houghton and Amberley and across the Downs to Findon, Bramber, Beeding and eventually Shoreham. Charles did of course venture into East Sussex through Portslade and into Brighton where he spent his last night on English soil for over nine years (but we'll leave that for *Visitors' Historic Britain: East Sussex*).

If you want to follow Charles' route through West Sussex, then we need to start at Racton, north-west of Chichester again. Racton Park Farm today contains the last remains of Racton Manor House, originally a Tudor house which is where Charles' loyal lieutenant, Colonel George Gunter of Racton, lived and who not only masterminded Charles' escape but organized his transport for freedom. The family is commemorated at the Gunter family tomb, built in 1624 and on display in the Church of St Peter, opposite where the manor house stood. The church also has other monuments celebrating the Gunter (or 'Gounter' as they are also known) family and a royal coat of arms celebrating the Colonel's service. Should that not be enough of a Civil War 'fix' for you, then the thatched cottage outside the church was once where Charles stayed, according to St Peter's Church website, but then, if we believe all the claims of where supposedly Charles slept, it is more places than Lenny Henry has filmed his Premier Inn commercials in. There is an effigy of a Gunter, but unfortunately it is the one who died in 1624, not the one who helped the monarch. It is amazing though to be in the homeplace of and chapel used by the man we have to credit for the saving of the Royal family—whether that is a good or a bad thing of course, is determined by the measure of republican or monarchist sentiment you possess. The other leading light in planning Charles' escape is the wonderfully-named Doctor Henchman of Salisbury Cathedral, who later became Bishop of Salisbury (so no longer a Henchman!). It is sad that Racton House no longer exists, but thankfully before it was demolished in 1830 Gunter's account of his journey with the 'Scottish King' (he had only been crowned in Scotland) was discovered, lodged into a small space in a bureau. Quite apt really, as Charles had himself been squeezed into some tight spaces too on his travels.

Gunter went on to accompany the 19-year-old Charles on his travels across the county with Charles originally travelling in disguise as Gunter's servant, his face blackened to create a look of poverty and his long locks shorn short. This prompted a clueless colleague of Gunter's to think the prince-in-disguise was in fact a Parliamentarian. Charles' two days in Sussex between October 13–15 in 1651 included a near miss in Arundel Forest, food in Houghton and a brush with Roundheads at Bramber. The town was full of soldiers, so perhaps emboldened by food and ale at Houghton, Gunter decided to bluff and the royal party on horseback boldly rode past Parliament's forces. As they approached Bramber bridge, however, fifty of the calvary rode at great speed towards them. There was nothing they could do but hold their breath—any attempt to gallop off would lead to the cavalry overtaking and capturing them; it seemed the escape had failed. Charles and company were able to breathe again as the Roundheads cantered right past them—on another mission. Once they'd crossed the bridge, Gunter left Charles with the rest of the party and galloped off to arrange Charles' escape over the sea to France and safety, and Charles' adventures would finally continue—but in what is now Brighton and Hove, before returning to West Sussex to set sail from Shoreham Harbour. The Monarch's Way is marked on maps and a series of books by Trevor Attrill (who coined the name of the route back in 1994) are available should you want to follow the route in great detail.

Lunch Locally: Pubs all over the south and west of England claim Charles stayed, or at least dined with them on his route, and those called the 'Royal Oak' signify the Rambling Royal's hiding from his pursuers in an oak tree, which, (although the actual one was at Boscobel in the West Midlands) again is celebrated across the country in numerous locations in one of Britain's most popular pub names. To experience eating places that benefitted from Charles II's cash after his restoration, you need to wait for *Visitors' Historic Britain: East Sussex*, such as the Royal Oak in Lewes or the Old Ship in Brighton. In the meantime, why not eat at the George And Dragon at Houghton, where you face down towards the bridge where Charles made his escape to freedom and where yes, surprise, surprise, apparently he stopped to rest or refresh. But who could blame him? As mentioned, it is a fantastic food pub with amazing views. Findon, where the Meandering Monarch passed through, is also blessed with great pubs such as The Gun and the Village House.

The political earthquake that was the Civil War threw up a realm of new political experiments and groups such as the Diggers and Levellers. The following Stuart era Mk II, the Restoration, which occurred following the end of the short-lived Cromwellian dynasty would instead see experiments in religion. Some stuck to the Catholicism that had helped cause the Civil War, whereas others who refused to follow Charles and James' Church of England followed non-conformist Protestant groups such as the Wesleyians, the Presbyterians, the Baptists and the Quakers. It is the Quakers that leave the greatest legacy in Sussex, with one of their group, William Penn, not only managing to attract 200 followers to meetings ten miles away from any large town, but the state of Pennsylvania and city of Philadelphia of course in America. This group is worthy of investigation not just because of the cruel treatment they attracted at this time in some cases (eggs and stones thrown at their meetings for starters, with a main course of whippings and imprisonment) but because they attracted ordinary farmers, labourers and Yeomen; any history of the county must tell the tale of ordinary folk, not just the Norfolks, Gorings, Percies and royalty. These ordinary Sussexians underwent hard times too for their peaceful beliefs; around 200 were imprisoned in Horsham Gaol alone, including a certain George Fox.

George Fox was the man who established the Quakers, or Society of Friends as they were also known. He first visited Sussex in 1655, three years after the Society was founded. By 1684, Fox's friend, William Penn was holding large meetings of converts at the **6. Blue Idol** near Coolham and at his home at Warminghurst Place, at the end of a narrow lane west of Ashington. The latter has been demolished, but the unusually-named Blue Idol is now part private dwelling and part Friends Meeting House. Penn was away in America but gave a fellow Quaker, John Shaw, the task of finding (and paying for!) a meeting place and the house known as 'Little Slatters' built around 1580 was their choice; a snip at the sum of £53 back in 1691, which Shaw bought on Penn's return. It wouldn't become known as the Blue Idol until the 1800s, by which time the Quakers were long gone. As was Penn. Surprisingly though, Penn didn't take to America, despite parts of it being founded by him and he returned to England, but not to Sussex; ending his days in Buckingham. Even more surprisingly, he named

Pennsylvania after his father, and Philadelphia is named to reflect the ethos of the Quakers, that of brotherly love—as opposed to war and conflict. There is also a memorial stone at nearby Thakeham marking where Penn used to stand and preach. The Blue Idol is today open for worship still and although the Quaker traditions are still remembered, the origins of the name of the meeting house are long forgotten. One theory is that the place was left idle for years and the whitewash between the Tudor beams was painted blue, another that there was a mysterious blue ceramic figure found in the garden. The mysterious name of this one-time pub is just one reason to go and see this fantastic building, another is that it is represents changing levels of religious tolerance in Britain. The Blue Idol was one of the first Quaker meeting houses in the country, following the religious Toleration Act of 1691, the year this enigmatic house became a religious venue. Most importantly though, it is not often one gets to see the place one of the 'founding fathers' of America lived and worshipped at.

Sussex without Satnav: Our last location (if we ignore the Monarch's Way) was Albourne, so from Albourne to the Blue Idol in Old House Lane, we need to head north back up the B2118, north up to A23 London-bound and then turn off west at the A272 (Petersfield/Midhurst direction). Turn off northwards at Dragons Lane up Bakers Lane in the direction of Southwater and then you come into Old House lane, the old house in question being the Blue Idol. It's worth contacting the Blue idol via their website first as they do welcome visitors inside the house if you do, otherwise it is only open Fridays March–November or Sundays for worship. Moving to Petworth next, come back down onto the A272 and head West—the A272 passes through the town and the house is easily signposted.

After the decade of demolition that was the Civil Wars was over, the Restoration led to a restoration of the country's finances and subsequently a continuation of the building of great houses as we move from seventeenth century into the early eighteenth.

Uppark and Petworth are both from the later Stuart era and, as we have seen, both experienced capture and recapture in that great Stuart sideshow, the Civil Wars. We start with **7. Petworth House**, where the current house

Petworth House

(built between 1688–96) is probably the fourth great house built on the site, with a previous house's thirteenth-century chapel still in existence inside. The 6th Duke of Somerset gained the previous thirteenth-century manor house by marriage and it was he that rebuilt the house into the grand current building, retaining only the chapel. Petworth's glorious front was due to be continued to the rear, but was only partly 'wrapped around' and so the rear of the house has a wonderfully higgledy-piggledy look of an earlier era of housebuilding.

It is the front of Petworth House juxtaposed with its grounds that make Petworth unique; the size, symmetry and length of the house, reflected across the water of the lake, all in a park designed to look as if it is natural, when in fact it was all man-made. At a time when gardens had been carefully coiffured, Capability Brown took pleasure in making landscapes look effortlessly natural, so the way the parkland touches the house, means it looks a rude intrusion into a wild and rugged almost moorland landscape. Which somehow seems right; the style of house and its grounds look more like it should be somewhere in Yorkshire, with Brontë characters parading around. The 600–700 wild deer at the park take us away even further and add a sense of the plains of Europe to the setting. This all means the park at Petworth adds value to any visit, not just due to its setting for so many landscapes by Turner, or its creation by Lancelot 'Capability' Brown (so called as he would say early in his career that every new site had 'capability'), but also due to the historic tales it tells. Like Parham,

Petworth had a road through it diverted, but also more than that, there were much older stables in the ground and the remains of a much older building that archaeologists are still puzzled as to its function and the reasons why such a grand building would be demolished. It may even be that the older versions of Petworth House weren't on the current site and are elsewhere in the grounds of the current magnificent house.

8. Uppark, or 'Up-Park' as it was earlier known, is so called due to the steep road you take to this small but perfectly formed mansion and its breathtaking grounds, with views of the sea and borderland Sussex. The Duke of Wellington was mistaken to turn down the offer of this estate, which he declined due to the steepness of the approach road (he claimed that climbing the Alps had been enough for him). Uppark's lofty position is what makes the house unique in Sussex, as is the fact its three main Wren era fronts have not been altered since its construction in 1685–90, believed to be by William Talman. It is certainly a case in point of how architectural styles were differing at this time, compared to the Tudor era, when you compare Uppark with Petworth, both of which were completed in the same year; Uppark proudly displays what Pevsner calls its 'Dutch parentage'. Edwarde Forde, its first owner, took the side of William of Orange against James II and was rewarded with a prominent position in society. When we visit, despite the 1989 fire, we are rewarded with a building from the age of William and Mary but an interior that is of the eighteenth century.

The building may look Dutch on the outside, but its location is anything but similar to Holland's flat fields, due to its elevated vantage point of the English Channel. You can see why Edward Forde, the first Earl of Tankerville who it was built for, would choose such a location, and why the Featherstonehaugh family were keen to buy it off him in 1747. Making sure a building at such high altitude on the crest of the Downs was awash with water was no problem as Forde had been responsible for the first public water supply into London in 1690. Sir Matthew and Lady Sarah Featherstonehaugh (sometimes pronounced as 'Fanshawe') would turn the house into a trophy case for their collection they'd amassed on their Grand Tour of Europe. The house was enjoyed in a different way during the time of their son, Sir Harry Featherstonehough, who used it as a party house for the Great and Good in society, including the Prince Regent and Emma Hamilton (she was still Emma Hart at that time and Featherstonehaugh's mistress at the age of 15). Emma Hamilton, who is said to have danced naked on a table at one of Uppark's parties, would of course go on to scandalously be Nelson's mistress. Uppark was no stranger to scandal later on either, as Harry at the age of 70 married the house's dairymaid, Mary Anne Bullock. This time the age difference was much greater, and Mary a tad older at the age of either 20 or 27, depending on which report you read. We doubt Sir Harry, as a one-time member of the infamous Hellfire club, would have been bothered what age Bullock was. Mary Anne Bullock may have been of lowly birth compared to her husband, but she and her sister who lived on at Uppark after his death were responsible for ensuring the house was kept in its eigthteenth century guise as 'Sir 'Arry' would have wanted it and avoided the Victorian 'improvements' many houses such as Parham faced.

Another servant of Uppark would go on to great things but through her son, H.G. Wells, who grew up in the house where his mother worked as housekeeper from 1880. His exploration of Uppark's subterranean tunnels under the house as a youngster are said to have helped inspire him to write *The Time Machine*, usually considered Wells' best book. The situation between the gentle Eloi, who live above ground and are descendants from the aristocracy and the dark-loving Morlocks, who evolved from the servant classes is believed to be inspired by his time at Uppark where his mother's quarters were below ground. In *The Time Machine*, ventilation shafts link upper and lower worlds, similar to the upper and lower levels at Uppark. You can still see these today as you explore the tunnels, where a number of dark bats roost and pretend you are in the realm of the Morlocks. They take you to the dairy where Sir Harry met his milkmaid and the stables where the house's horses lived. The house is also reflected in Wells' semi-autobiographical novel, *Tono-Bungay* as Bladesover. H.G. Wells owed a debt to Uppark for keeping his family from the workhouse when his father was not able to work as a cricketer by providing his mother employment and for inspiring his work. He was also allowed access to its library, and so this boy who was forced to leave school and undertake menial jobs gained a self-education this way. We therefore owe a debt to Uppark too.

Uppark (below) thankfully survived the disastrous fire of 1989, which was broadcast around the world, and quite apt for the house that the writer of *The Time Machine* lived in, the National Trust, with the choice of restoring it to its seventeenth century beginnings or eighteenth century heyday decided to turn back the clock to restore it to…the day before the fire. The restoration was sumptuous, however, and makes us want more ruined buildings to be restored—why not Cowdray? A visit to Uppark means not just a visit to one of Sussex's most historic houses, but the chance to play the game of what is and what is not original. Even the restoration now provides us with a link to a twentieth century historic event as one of the masons involved in its repair carved upon one of the restored chimneys: 'Margaret Thatcher resigned as I was making this.'

Sussex without Satnav: We started this chapter at the west of the county and we end up back there as this part of the book is going chronologically rather than easterly. From Petworth, continue west on the A272 until you come to Elsted Road. Take this until you reach Uppark.

Lunch Locally: Uppark has a rather wonderful tea room that is great for hungry folk of all ages. The view out of the windows is marvellous and the food is generous and scrumptious. Why go anywhere else? Well, there is the Three Horseshoes in Elsted if you're thirsting for the wider range of drinks at a gorgeous pub.

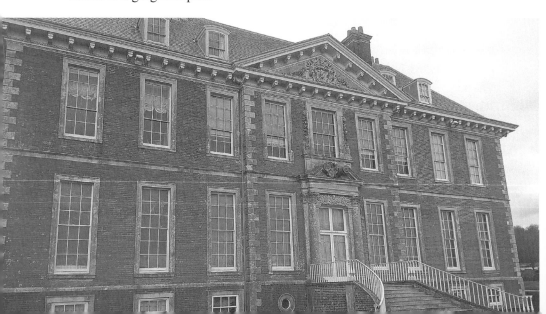

CHAPTER 8

Georgian, Napoleonic and Regency Sussex

'Georgian' and 'Regency' are combined here as the Regency era is technically part of the Georgian Age, the Regent in question being the Prince Regent, who would become George IV (1820–1830). Prince George became Regent between 1811–1820 when George III was judged unfit to rule due to mental illness, although he had wanted to be Regent much earlier during previous bouts of his father's insanity. Technically the Georgian era starts in 1714 and the Regency follows from 1811–20, but we don't tend to use 'Georgian' as a description after that, despite the Regent becoming yet another George when on the throne after 1820. Nor do we use it when two more Georges take the throne in the twentieth century. 'Georgian' is, however, applied to the whole of the eighteenth century, and 'Regency' has been used to apply to the whole reign of George IV as well as 1811–21 before, and for later developments into the 1840s. The Regency-style of development is succeeded by the Italianate style in Brighton as shown in Brighton's 1840s Park Crescent and Montpelier Crescent at Seven Dials, built in the 1840s and finished by 1855 by Brighton's eminent architect, Amon Henry Wilds. There is often confusion over the use of the term 'Regency' therefore. One hotel in Sussex recently referred to its 1860s-built hotel as 'Regency' on its website!

The Georgian era is another great housebuilding era, and we also see the first large-scale house developments such as crescents, and squares but these are not to be found in West Sussex. The fan of this era needs to explore London and, nearer to home, Brighton for good examples, which we will look at in *Visitors' Historic Britain: East Sussex*. West Sussex has a range of Georgian development in Arundel, Horsham and Chichester, which all experienced much rebuilding of Tudor and Stuart town buildings at this time, or at least the changing of facades of buildings so the front of shops and houses gained a Georgian makeover. For the grandest urban collection of Georgian buildings, then a trip to St Martin's Square in Chichester is recommended. Georgian builds can show great symmetry, but can also be much more higgledy-piggledy than later Regency-style building developments—a good case in point being the rambling Bedford Row in Worthing from which building commenced in 1803 or Montague Place, dating back to the late 1700s when compared to the later and much more orderly 1820s Liverpool Terrace to the north.

The most famous Regency Building (which will be featured in *Visitors' Historic Britain: East Sussex*) Brighton's Royal Pavilion started its Indianesque makeover (it has undergone two already) in the Regency era but wasn't finished until into George's reign in 1822. That was in turn inspired by a design in Georgian times by Repton, not Nash at all (he merely changed and elaborated Repton's designs), and Repton's designs took their cues from Porden's riding stables (the Dome and Corn Exchange today), begun in 1803. So then, by the phrase 'Regency style' (which is perhaps more accurate) we take our cues from Regent's Street in London, with liberal applications of sash or bow (round) windows, pillars and brickwork largely hidden by the covering of stucco, painted cream today. Liverpool Terrace in Worthing is a good example of this and when venturing into Brighton, we see of course Regency and Brunswick Squares, The Royal Albion Hotel. By Victoria's era though, tastes had changed to more Italianate design, as shown by Hove's Palmeira Square and its surrounds. Sash windows were converted into more angular bay windows by the Victorians, as were even some bow windows.

Born before and developed within the Georgian era to the west of the country is a great example of a house that breathes the Georgian era. **1. Goodwood** has had a house on its current site since the 1530s it seems and the current house dates from the Jacobean era, but it was in 1697 that Charles II's illegitimate son, the Duke of Richmond, purchased the house as a hunting lodge. Either he or his successor expanded the small house with gabled ends and an extension to the south. It is the 3rd Duke of Richmond who is the most important owner of the house though, extending and rebuilding the north wing. The Richmonds' other property, Richmond House in London, burnt down and so Goodwood became the home of the family art collection, which it remains today, ten generations later. The house under the 3rd Duke took most of its present form between 1780–1800 from designs from Wyatt and Nash, so it not only contains art, but these leading architects ensured the building is a piece of art, set in the middle of a 12,000-acre canvas.

It isn't just art that Goodwood is known for today; the house is an epicentre of thrills and spills on land and air, and not too far away from the sea either. It is the home of the Goodwood Revival and Festival of Speed, events that we think have gone on forever in Sussex, but were only created by the current Earl of March and Kinrara (whose father is still the current Duke), in the 1990s. His grandfather was the one who created the airfield that would become Westhampnett in the Second World War, part of the chain of airfields protecting Sussex from invasion in 1940. Goodwood makes us look up not just at aircraft still today, but at the hills where the 3rd Duke laid out the Goodwood racecourse that still gives us 'Glorious Goodwood' today every July, when the horsepower in focus is that of the actual horse and not the combustion-engine produced kind. Power of a different kind was needed in the grounds of Goodwood in the 1930s to help the then Duke of Richmond pay his taxes. Just under 100,000 beech trees were sold in roughly ten minutes, the biggest sale of timber ever in the country. Today people from all over come to visit and participate in this playground of pleasure, whose origins date back to the pleasures of Charles II and his mistress, Louise de Kérouaille. It is apt that a house bought and developed by Charles II's descendants had the Rambling Royal pass through the grounds of Goodwood on his escape to Brighton during the Civil War.

2. Castle Goring - The Georgian and Regency eras used different architectural styles. Castle Goring, west of Goodwood on the A27 into Worthing, celebrates this with the use of the Gothic on its north front, designed to replicate the medieval style of Arundel Castle and the classical to the south, said to be an homage to the famous Villa Lante near Rome. It even has a corridor that starts off in the gothic style one end and ends up in the classical, Greco-Roman style at the other. This is one of the things that makes Castle Goring so particularly 'astonishing' as Nairn said in *The Buildings of England* guide to Sussex. Buildings with two very different styles of frontage are usually those where a later wing was built onto an earlier wing from a previous century whereas this little-known stately home, visited by Queen Victoria in the early years of her reign, is deliberately built in this Gemini-style. This is probably due to the fact that the building was a collaboration between Sir Bysshe Shelley, of the local landowning family, and local architect responsible for several great Worthing buildings, John Biagio Rebecca. It was the only building the Shelley family ever commissioned, making it more special. Rebecca also designed other local buildings such as St Paul's and Beach House in Worthing, which you can see hints of on the south-facing side. However, it is the northern, crenellated front which is the most romantic, as befitting for the house's planned first owner.

Bysshe Shelley built the house not for his son, Sir Timothy Shelley, but for his grandson, the poet Percy Bysshe Shelley at a cost of £90,000 between 1790 and 1805. Had the famous poet not drowned in Italy at the age of 29, he was due to be the house's first inhabitant. Instead, his wife Mary Shelley, the famous author behind 'Frankenstein' sold the mansion. It is amazing to think what it would have been like as the home of this amazing literary couple and their offspring. Castle Goring's fate instead was transition between owners until it came into possession of the Somerset family. They held onto it for 170 years including a period of less-than-caring treatment by Canadian soldiers billeted in the Second World War. The house never really recovered from this and was further neglected during its time as a language school. By the time author, socialite and reality television personality Lady Colin Campbell purchased the building in 2013 for £700,000 it needed over £2m pounds worth of repairs, especially to the roof which had had £50,000 worth of its lead stolen in a 2012 break-in. Walls were crumbling and numerous windows had been smashed. Famously appearing on *I'm a Celebrity, Get Me Out Of Here!* in 2015 to raise funds to repair the house and stop the now-leaking roof, this guardian angel stepped in at the eleventh hour to save this wonderful building, which had been placed as a Grade A priority; the top of English Heritage's list of buildings needing emergency action to save their architectural features and historic value. 'Lady C' as she has become known to her many fans is now the genial hostess at many functions at the house, including a New Year's Eve event where you can see the new year in with the saviour of this unique building. The building is now happily a successful conference event and especially a wedding venue, with increasing numbers of bookings following the televised story of Lady Colin's challenge of restoring the building in time for its first event. Sussex is indeed incredibly lucky to have this 15,600ft^2 architecturally-schizophrenic Georgian masterpiece (one of the two Grade I listed buildings in Worthing) and most important houses architecturally this nation possesses just off the A27.

Sussex without Satnav: Apparently not really needed here at first but tricky by the end by car. You just get back onto the A27 at Chichester from Goodwood and head east. Castle Goring is on the south side of the A27 so you will need to continue into West Worthing junction and take a U-turn when safe to. Castle Goring isn't signposted and is hidden from the A27 by trees in the summer so don't go as far as the turnoff to Angmering/ Littlehampton as you head back westwards along the A27. From Castle Goring to the Worthing locations below, continue briefly east on the A27, take the West Worthing turning at the junction at the top of the slip road off the A27 and this will take you down Titnore Lane. At the Swallow's Return roundabout, take the first exit onto the A259 and follow the signs to the centre of Worthing. It's always more cheerful parking on the seafront in Worthing rather than the grotty multi-storey car parks if you can!

George IV's visits to Brighton are the most famous example of royal patronage helping a struggling Sussex settlement rediscover itself, but his younger sister Amelia played a role in establishing the new seaside resort of Worthing on the map. Up until 1798, Worthing had been a smattering of buildings focussed around the site of the Swan Inn today, near Waitrose and increasingly, around the sea end of South Street where Worthing Pier is today. George's youngest sister, who was 15 was suffering, not from the glands like her elder brother (probably more likely to be his overeating), but from swollen knees and so a seawater cure was deemed just the ticket. Taking her to Brighton meant steeper, unsteady beaches though and the possibility of corruption by her older brother's nefarious company and parties. George III instead decreed that his youngest daughter would experience the flatter, sandier beaches of the new resort of Worthing where she could get into the sea easier and keep away from naughty George. At this time **3. Warwick House**, owned by Edward Ogle, the town's leading commissioner, was the primary holiday 'let' for the wealthy (despite it never having a bathroom in its 120-year existence) with its prime location north of what is today Worthing's Steyne. It seems, however, that Amelia stayed in Worthing's only terrace of town houses at this time, **4. Montague Place**, which had been built in the 1700s but had recently been rebuilt. George apparently visited up to fifteen times and wasn't impressed with the standard of accommodation for little sis, but records show she was right next to the sea, which Montague Place was then and so the poorly princess could be carried much easier to the briny from there. Wherever Amelia stayed Worthing, which had only had its first recorded visitor in the 1750s, soon received other visitors from the worlds of royalty and writing, with Jane Austen staying in a smaller residence, **5. Stanford's Cottage** in 1805 for several months. She was inspired to use Worthing as her basis for the being-constructed town that Worthing was in 1805 when *Sanditon* was incompletely written in 1817, and it would be interesting to know if, like any of her other novels that she attempted much earlier than their publication date, early drafts were ever written in Worthing as she experienced similar events.

Despite Amelia's boost to the town's fortunes, there is little to celebrate Worthing's first royal visitor. Montague Place has no blue plaque, due to the uncertainty of where exactly Amelia stayed, but at least it wasn't demolished and built over with a housing development in the late 1800s as Warwick House (which Amelia would have been likely to visit) was. The late Edwardian housing estate does at least have a replacement Warwick House, built by the builder of the development. There is an office block named after her in Crescent Road and the Council finally named a green space 'Amelia Park' to celebrate the centenary of the visit. The semi-crescent of houses, designed by Amon Henry Wilds, surrounding Amelia Park, **6. Park Crescent** (originally Royal Park Crescent) is a worthy visit for fans of Regency Style architecture or of the Wilds and Busby firm of architects, as this is the only development of these prolific Brighton architects and echoes their later Park Crescent built at the north end of what is now Brighton's Level park and Wilds' Montpelier Crescent development in Brighton. It is even more unusual as, like another large Worthing development from the nineteenth century, the Chatsworth Hotel terrace, is incomplete; it was planned to be a full crescent, but funding likewise became a problem in the turbulent economic times of the early 1830s. Building, which commenced in 1831, ceased promptly in 1833. The Beechwood Hall Hotel, originally the Swiss Cottages, was due to be a free-standing building in the centre of the Crescent and grand villas would be abutting what is now Richmond Road. Montpelier Crescent looked up at the Downs from Brighton when first built, and Park Crescent in Brighton down to St Peter's Church, but on the same altitude as more southerly developments in Worthing, it is unclear what Wilds was hoping the end effect of Worthing's Park Crescent would be and it is strange that he didn't try to recreate his Father's Kemp Town or Brunswick in Brighton and Hove along the much emptier seafront at Worthing at this time, but instead somewhere with an obstructed sea view. Nevertheless, Park Crescent in Worthing is a rare architectural gem in Worthing and a good example of Italianate building from Brighton's premier architectural firm.

Sussex without Satnav: Best to leave the car parked when you get to Worthing as it's all flat, close and walkable. Montague Place is directly off the seafront at Worthing, near the Pier and Warwick Place was where the houses and shops are now behind the 'Broadway' black and white set of buildings from 1901 at the north end of the Steyne. For Park Crescent, to get the best approach visually through its archway, it's best to walk west along the seafront to West Buildings and head north away from the sea. This becomes Crescent Road and you pass pleasant Victorian villas and Sion School on your left until you reach a small roundabout. Turn left and you'll see Park Crescent.

Lunch Locally: Worthing has a wealth of local and usually independently-owned eating places. Montague Place has a range of places to nibble and Warwick Street, near to where Warwick House was, has a pedestrianized plethora of Worthing places to chow down at. There is even a Warwick pub, but the Egremont opposite Warwick Place, a delightful

Georgian row of fishermen's cottages, which is practically a village within Worthing, might be a better bet. The Beechwood Hall Hotel in Amelia Park serves food and is halfway across where the completed crescent would have been.

The eighteenth century and early nineteenth seems to be the era of uncompleted developments that had a purpose and also completed developments that had no definite purpose. This era saw a craze for building follies and odd buildings in Sussex, as it was an age where not just your house, but what your grounds said about you were in focus. Several Sussex homebuilders and owners died in bankruptcy as they lived way beyond their means and the building of showy follies contributed to this. Wealthy Georgians felt under pressure to show off their wealth in weird and wonderful ways, of which we are the beneficiaries, even if we are sometime mystified by the purpose of some of these buildings or even what message the builders were trying to impart.

We start with the **7. Vandalian Tower**, returning to the far west of the county in part of the great grounds at Uppark. Built by Sir Matthew Featherstonehaugh of Uppark—his son Harry and the Prince Regent would use the octagonal Tower to continue their parties from an even higher viewpoint than the house. According to David Arscott in *Curiosities of West Sussex*, they would eat and drink to excess so much there that servants would be needed to carry them back down the hill in wheelbarrows.

There was much to celebrate about the Tower, so you can see why the Regent and his rakish chum would party to excess. It was designed to be another method of displaying the wealth and status of the Featherstonehaughs as part of their Capability Brown-designed grounds, but it also tells the tale of Sir Harry's father's role in the planned development of the failed 'state' of Vandalia in America. Sir Matthew had numerous commercial interests in America and with his business partners hoped to celebrate the heritage of the ruling Hanoverians as Queen Charlotte, George III's wife, was said to be descended from the East German tribe, the Vandals. A German tribe was the inspiration for the name of a new territory, that would be bought off a native American tribe. Featherstonehaugh and Co had purchased land off the Iroquois Indians in West Virginia, believing it would be a successful new state. The Tower was built to celebrate this new land and Sir Matthew's shrewd business dealing in creating it. The territory was good; the timing less so with Sir Matthew dying in 1774 and the War of Independence breaking out in 1775 to put an end to the new embryonic state. The land became part of the new independent American lands; which meant that overseas British landowners now owned nothing. The British government didn't want to know but the Featherstonehaughs certainly weren't ruined as Sir Harry would inherit vast wealth still, much of which he used for gambling, partying and purchasing of fine art. Even if the war had not broken out it was unlikely Vandalia would have worked as the new state was vociferously opposed by neighbouring Pennsylvania and Virginia. Vandalia ended up merged into being part of West Virginia and Kentucky. Slightly more exists of the Tower which, despite being consumed by flames in 1842, is a Grade II listed building.

Sussex without Satnav: Take the A286 and then the B2141 north-west out of Chichester from the ring road to get a good view of it—drive easterly along the B2141 from the east or on foot it can be accessed from the South Downs Way. To access Vandalia Tower directly you need to enter Uppark House and Gardens via Harting, so follow earlier directions. Otherwise, on the B2141 there is a National Trust car park, which costs £2 unless you're a National Trust member or blue badge holder. The best direction is by approaching from the east. For Upperton from the B2141, head south-east back down that road, take Binderton Lane until it becomes the A286 and then turn left and up the A286 until you take the shortcut east via Mill Lane to the A272. Tillington is just north off the A272 and north of that is Upperton. The 'Monument' is visible as you drive between Tillington and Lurgashall, or if you visit the Petworth House and grounds.

Lunch Locally: As mentioned earlier, the Horse Guards Inn at Tillington is well worth a visit as a quintessentially charming rural English inn. Petworth has several good 'eateries' too.

8. The Upperton Monument despite its name isn't strictly a monument, but more of a habited folly within, but on the edge of Petworth Park. Being

Above and below: *Hiorne Tower*

called a 'monument' suggests it commemorates something or someone, which it doesn't. It comprises a square tower, with an elongated turret sticking up from its middle rather like someone giving the middle finger gesture. It is worthy of a visit as, unlike the nearby Pitshill Tower (another folly), it is in better repair and you can actually reach it. As you would expect from somewhere within Petworth's grounds, it was sketched and also painted (in the distance) by Turner, when it would have been only a few decades old, having been built approximately about 1800. It is believed it was painted so that, as with much else in Petworth's grounds, there was a focal point for you to look at or walk towards in the north-east direction of the house.

9. Hiorne Tower in the grounds of Arundel Castle is unusual in being a triangular building. Its gothic and austere look provides the perfect backdrop for any horror movie setting, but most of all because of the wonderful walk a visit to it can entail. Those wanting to make their way to the Tower have a choice of starts; the first being to park near Arundel Cathedral and take the top route via the Cricket Ground to end up at the folly. The more energetic but impressive approach is to start again at the cathedral and walk around the castle grounds until you reach Swanbourne Lake and then navigate around this, climbing the hill in beautiful Arundel Park, leaving a natural beauty behind you for a more frowning and brooding man-made construction.

The man in question was Francis Hiorne, fellow of the Society of Antiquities and dedicated builder of churches and other properties across the country. Hiorne built the tower as an advert for his abilities as both builder and architect between 1789–90, on the orders of Charles Howard, 11th Duke of Norfolk, who was the instigator of a large number of redevelopments and improvements to Arundel Castle. The Duke seems to have commissioned the construction as a hunting lodge, although it seems like another hunting lodge owned by the castle's owners at one time, Amberley Castle, it was also lived in, although not by any of the Dukes. The Tower was his last sole project and today stands forlorn and alone, the odd window cracked or smashed. If it wasn't on the Norfolks' land, this no doubt would be the centrepiece of some small village of housing development. However, had the land around the Tower been developed, then it probably wouldn't have been used as the location for an episode of *Doctor Who* filmed there featuring the Cybermen back in 1988.

Follies were the stuff of fun and fashion, whereas lying across both the Georgian and Regency eras were the intermittent Revolutionary and Napoleonic Wars with France (1792–1815). East Sussex and Kent have more physical reminders of these wars, but Sussex has the Chichester and Wey and Arun canals, partly built so that gold bullion could be transported from the Bank of England to the fleet at Portsmouth to finance expeditions without risking its capture by privateers off the coast of England. West Itchenor's boatyards supplied ships for the many clashes at sea during this era, and Beacon Hill at South Harting was the location of a telegraph station but West Sussex's biggest legacy from these wars are the Nelson and Trafalgar-named streets and pubs. Once the Napoleonic Wars and its following economic turmoil were behind it, Sussex enjoyed a period of general prosperity and peace as the county enjoyed industrialization in the Victorian Age with its developments in resorts and railways. It is to this era we now turn.

CHAPTER 9

Industrial, Victorian, Resort and Railway Era Sussex

Unlike other areas of the UK, Sussex wasn't built on the wealth of the Industrial Revolution. Its grand terraces, squares and crescents were funded by the landed and investors capitalizing on the boom in visitors to the county's coastline. Its grand country houses were built on the profits from agriculture. Sussex had had its Industrial age when Manchester

Arundel

Arundel Cathedral

and Birmingham barely existed, which means that our countryside had recovered by the time the Industrial Revolution occurred and having no coal seams meant our landscape was left largely alone. Being close to London and en route to the Continent, Sussex experienced only two aspects of the Industrial Revolution: the growth of powered transport, especially the railways and sprawling urbanization, to provide for the boom in tourism and those who supported it. Sussex's second industrial age is really that of the Victorian era; its money was in farming, fun and being fashionable before that at the seaside. This means our buildings from this age are sometimes seemingly not of that age at all, with Arundel Cathedral, Lancing College Chapel and the private chapel at Arundel Castle all being Victorian homages to the Middle Ages that have fooled many as to their true age.

1. Arundel Cathedral or the Roman Catholic Cathedral of Our Lady and St Philip Neri (to give it its full title) was built between 1869 and 1873 on the orders of Henry, the 15th Duke of Norfolk. It is faced with Bath stone and built in a grandiose fifteenth century French Gothic style. It serves to complement the parish church just down the road which benefitted from a restoration just over a decade later. This dual arrangement may seem strange, but Arundel is the seat of the Bishopric of Arundel and Brighton, and since its creation in 1965, Arundel Cathedral has fulfilled the role of cathedral of the diocese. A cathedral it may be, but it was never completed; plans for a spire over the North Porch never came into being. This doesn't spoil the experience at all for the visitor; you enter into a world of light and spaciousness, illuminated by the stunning rose stained glass window. The cathedral has six magnificent pointed arches which divide the aisles from the nave, each a length of 97ft and a width of 33ft across. Each of the aisle are 12ft wide, making the visitor look up to the vaulted nave ceiling, which is decorated with carved foliage. The journey to the cathedral is also a magnificent one; whether walking upwards through Arundel's steep streets or first seeing the town from the bypass, you feel that you are in a part of France. The summit of Arundel is like nowhere else in Sussex and the rarity of a catholic cathedral makes a trip to Arundel for its cathedral a unique experience. Following a visit to the cathedral, it is well worth the walk past the cricket ground to Hiorne Tower, and on your return to enjoy a leisurely drink and a bite at St Mary's Gate Inn next door. Should you wish to leave your car behind for the day and enjoy more than one, it would be fitting to get a cab. This isn't just due to the dangers of drink-driving, but also because the cathedral has links with taxis. The building can claim the same designer as the Hansom Cab, both being designed by Joseph Hansom.

Moving eastwards once more from the Arun to the Adur, **2. Lancing College Chapel** is also amazing as the world's biggest school chapel and a building that has been continuing in its construction since its first plans were drawn in 1848. 'Some atonement for many heaps of ugliness,' the architectural critics Nairn and Pevsner said of Lancing College as a whole. Some atonement indeed, with nearly 170 years of work on this masterpiece that still isn't completed. The building started to be built not until six years after the plans were drawn and the death of the architect, R.C. Carpenter, in 1855 a year later didn't stop the project. The building work continued, and the first boys were admitted in 1858. R.C.'s son, R.H. Carpenter, continued his father's work and building began in 1868, reaching partial

Lancing College Chapel in a less-finished state

completion finally not until 1911. The school buildings continued being developed into the 1930s, and the Chapel, which was missing one nave, finally got this in 1962 due to a third and final Carpenter, R.C. Carpenter's third son, Billy. The college was one of fifteen independent schools, set up by the Reverend Nathaniel Woodard, that aimed to bring boys of all classes together in education. R.C. designed and built both school and chapel for Woodard, and Sussex's own Sagrada Família is also a huge achievement in terms of its construction. Its base was a mix of flint and clay so the huge necessary foundations needed to be drilled down 60ft to the solid chalk underneath. This family project was also huge—only Westminster Abbey, Liverpool Cathedral and York Minster manage to top Lancing's 145ft. Lancing College Chapel is still asking for donations to complete the West Porch of the chapel. It was hoped at one point that the Chapel would be connected to the school buildings, but this was rejected as impractical.

The railway is our main Industrial feature and though our railway manufacturing yards at Brighton and Lancing have long been demolished we are left with the mighty **3. Ouse Valley Viaduct at Balcombe**, and the **4. Clayton Tunnel North Portal**.

The latter's rather grand-sounding name basically refers to the entrance to the southbound tunnel under Clayton Hill that serves the London to Brighton railway line, near Hassocks Railway Station. The station (originally called Hassocks Gate) was built in 1841. As the last rural stopping place before the Downs it meant the village became a stopping point for those who wanted to explore the Downs. Before long, however, ladies of the oldest profession soon provided a service in the countryside nearby for those wanting to explore other sights. Hassocks today is a quiet village that has homed a surprising range of important people including Magnus Volk's family in the early 1900s, but it is the village of Clayton that has the more interesting historical and cultural sites, including its medieval church as well as the claim that *Doctor Who* was once filmed nearby with the magnificent Downs behind as its backdrop. The buildings that stand above the entrance to the tunnel at Clayton are the most inspiring and unusual buildings in the area, mainly due to the wonderfully eccentric idea of building a mock medieval castle above part of the Victorian domain of the railways.

Parents who have read their children the wonderful book *Shhh!* will be reminded of the Giant's castle on first seeing the tunnel's entrance; a gaping dark chasm of a mouth awaiting those about to enter. You almost expect to see the Railway Children running from it, so much are you transported to another century and the world of fiction. Despite looking like a castle, the Grade II buildings above the tunnel's mouth in 1841 also include perched atop of it when you look closer the tunnel keeper's cottage, built eight years later. The residents of this ever since then are the only ones in Sussex to have a railway line running directly under their front room, continuing deep below up to a maximum of 270ft of chalk hillside above. The tunnel was described in its steam-filled heyday by Charles G Harper in *The Brighton Road* in 1922 as 'continually vomiting steam and smoke, like a hell's mouth' and was also the location of a horrific crash in 1861 twenty years after the line opened, which was the worst rail disaster of its time, killing twenty-three people and severely injuring many more. It is also one of two railway disasters to have inspired a story by Dickens, *The Signalman*, the other being the Staplehurst Rail Crash, which Dickens was personally involved in. The Clayton Tunnel crash is also said to be the reason, unsurprisingly, that the Portal is said to be haunted still today, although the noises that plague the cottages to this day could be simply the local wildlife scurrying along its underground secret tunnel and passage.

Those not interested in the supernatural may still want to visit for its beautiful use of yellow brick and Caen stone detail and for the fact that it was built by Balcombe Viaduct and Brighton Station architect, David Mocatta. The fact Mocatta built both Brighton Station and the Portal might answer the still-debated reason such a magnificent building was constructed over a railway tunnel. Perhaps we can see the buildings as an extended gatehouse to Mocatta's station building; a statement that you are entering the area of 'Greater Brighton'—a great railway city? This is supported by the strange fact that there is no equivalent building for those leaving Brighton at the south end of the tunnel—the building there is very simple. The very different building styles of Brighton Station and the Clayton Tunnel entrance however make this 'gatehouse' theory less viable. Other theories have included that building a construction reminiscent of England's past would reassure those using such a modern method of transport as the railways at that time hurtled towards the black abyss of Clayton Tunnel. Another is that it is a commemoration of the one-and-a-quarter mile tunnel, marvellously carved through the chalk hillside by the 6,000 men who laboured on this engineering masterpiece. It certainly deserves celebrating as the longest tunnel on the London to Brighton line. An alternative idea is that such a grand edifice, costing £90,000 back in 1841, placated the local landlord who like many at the time was unsure about the railways carving through his land.

Whatever its beginnings, the tunnel still provokes interest and fascination today, and has inspired many memorable quotes including being called: 'A spectacular, castellated and turreted confection of light stone' by the *Daily Telegraph*. *Sussex Living* described it as 'A place of opposites, suspended between myth and modernity', whereas the *Daily Express* was less complimentary, calling the 1849 building merely: 'Anorak Cottage'. Clayton Tunnel and its magnificent masterpiece of a tunnel entrance are far more than this; a visit to this fantastic folly can also include a walk through Clayton, a romp up the Downs to the Jack and Jill Windmills and finished off with a supper and drinks at the nearby pub which is named after the windmills and is just across the lane from this terrific tunnel mouth. Who wouldn't want to visit such an eccentric building that has a delicious sense of irony and ridiculousness in that it is a building that looks like a fortress but due to a great big hole in it can be entered so easily.

As we move northwards up the line, we cross the Ouse Valley Viaduct, a north-south rural counterpart to Sussex's other great railway viaduct, the east-west Rastrick's Viaduct across the Wellesbourne Valley that is the London Road into Brighton today. Although built five years apart, the two look similar as John Urpeth Rastrick also built the Balcombe Viaduct as the Ouse Valley Viaduct is also known. It was built in 1841 and it is hard to believe its thirty-seven semi-circular arches once crossed, only over 175 years ago, a River Ouse that was still just about navigable enough then to bring its eleven million bricks and stonework up the river to the construction site. Only a few miles from Haywards Heath, unlike its younger Brighton sister, the viaduct is a pretty picnic site still in open fields and you can explore the piers at your ease. Your peace and quiet is occasionally shattered by around 110 trains a day passing overhead on the

Brighton Main Line to and from London, but you half-expect the Hogwarts Express to pass by 90ft above you, being chased by Harry Potter and Ron Weasley in a flying Ford Anglia across the 450m span of the Grade II listed bridge.

The railway was only made possible by the technological changes of the Industrial era and railways meant the masses could reach Sussex easier. No longer an isolated, hard-to-reach and impenetrable part of the country, Sussex could now be reached in minutes, not endless hours or days. The railway industry would boom in Sussex; manufacturing, supply, staffing and repair but the railways also meant the age of the commuter. Those enjoying the economic benefits of coastal expansion could work there and still live in the country; and the same with the London-bound. This meant existing towns such as Horsham could expand and whole new settlements were established where stations had been built along the Brighton and other lines. These became known as the 'Mushroom' railway towns as they mushroomed quickly in growth: Burgess Hill and Haywards Heath are the two biggest, but Hassocks also grew as the last stop before the Downs and the place the Greensand Way intersected the London Road near to a new station. With all three, the place to see the early settlements are near the stations—the railway hotels and inns, early Victorian villas and other buildings are the nucleus of these new towns of the Victorian era. Should you wish to visit perhaps the most unusual memorial to the Railway Age then the grounds of Chichester Cathedral have a statue to William Huskisson, the city's one-time MP and the first person ever to be famously run over and killed by a steam engine.

Sussex had no coal to quarry so the landscape has remained relatively unharmed by the Industrial era compared with South Wales or the North, but it did have sand in limited places. Quarrying took place late on in the Industrial era and into the twentieth century in rural Washington and Storrington, along the A283 that we have travelled several times in this book, north of the Downs. At one point the roundabout at Washington was where a quarry was, and is said to be where a First World War tank is still buried to this day. Head south from here and the sand of the Weald turns to chalk which was useful in cement works, so huge sections of the Downs were carved out, north of South Heighton over in East Sussex and on a massive scale at the **5. Cement Works at Upper Beeding**. This mutilation of the Downs, Sussex's finest asset, would be impossible today but it means with the huge chalk quarry north of Shoreham we have a reminder of the late Industrial stage of Sussex's history. This quarry gave much wealth to the area, keeping many families of Beeding in employment until the First World War and remained open until 1991. It leaves us also the route of an industrial railway line that remained open until 1988 and was the final part of the Steyning Line between Shoreham and Christ's Hospital, closed in the Beeching Report, to remain open. The other, more spectral hangovers from this era are the cement works buildings at the quarry and across the road from it. No more horrific a set of buildings exists in Sussex, in terms of their lack of consideration for their rural environment, or their blight of one of Sussex's more scenic river valleys. The buildings of the cement works seem to even play with reality; they seem so unreal as to be CGI animation, or the lair of a Bond villain, whose model form would be destroyed at the finale of a Bond movie, Sean Connery and accomplice having made their way to its inner sanctum and set the complex to self-destruct. Before the planned destruction or rejuvenation of the buildings takes place, Beeding Cement Works is crying out to be used as a film set.

This was originally also the Shoreham to Partridge Green line, but even after Dr Beeching's cuts of the 1960s and the closure of the passenger line, this railway continued as a goods line. You can only look at Beeding Cement works from the outside (or walk past it along the riverside walk that was once the railway line) but for a one-time quarry you can enter that celebrates all of Sussex's industrial past, then a visit to the **6. Amberley Museum & Heritage Centre** (previously called Amberley Working Museum) is an excellent way to spend a day amongst 36 acres dedicated to the industrial heritage of the south-east of England. Starting up in 1979, the museum is a hands-on place for all ages with numerous events all year long and has free heritage bus and train rides around its grounds. You can still see the lime kilns where lime would be made from the excavated chalk and if Sussex's industrial heritage throughout the years isn't enough for you, then you can see the entrance to one of Hollywood's most famous mines, the Mainstrike Mine from the 1985 Bond film *A View To A Kill*, where Amberley Museum stood in as a location for Silicon Valley in the USA

(Beachy Head in East Sussex also stood for the Rock of Gibraltar in *The Living Daylights*). There is so much at Amberley Museum to see and do that an entry ticket is good value (an annual pass even more so) but should you want to just see Sussex lime kilns, then there are some you can see for free off the Old London Road as you travel south from Washington village up towards the Washington Bostal. Take the rough road that winds east above the Old London Road and you can see the kilns that were fed with lime from the nearby quarry further south off the Bostal. These were a much smaller affair than the pits at 'Houghton and Bury' (as Amberley was known) as Washington had no nearby water to transport such products, which takes us onto one last Industrial era development in Sussex.

Unlike the industrial Midlands and North, Sussex had no coal to export, but it could export timber, manure, agricultural goods and from Amberley, lime. This is why the river at Amberley was diverted to create a port and other stretches of the Arun were altered. Without coalfields or a vast manufacturing base, Sussex had little need for canals, but the River Arun could be linked to a canal so that access by water was possible from London via the River Wey to sea. This is why today in Sussex we have two restored canals that can be visited: the Chichester Canal and the Wey and Arun north of the county around Loxwood. This wasn't the only investment in the county's network of waterways, as in the 1790s the 3rd Earl of Egremont of Petworth financed the development of the Rother navigation so that a canal would connect Petworth and Midhurst with the Arun, to improve the economic prowess of the area by boosting agricultural exports. There is not much to see of the eight locks and other improvements he built today, but you can see the **7. Chichester Canal** still, and the **8. Wey and Arun**, both of which are thriving with boat trips, volunteers and developments taking place to bring the original route from London to the sea back, hopefully one day into existence. It would be wonderful if once more you could get to London from the English Channel and these two canals which will be part of that route have played an important starting role.

Lunch Locally: The best place for a walk or to begin an exploration of the canal is probably the Onslow Arms in Loxwood High Street. This charming, cosy and welcoming pub provides you with a waterside garden for drinks or afternoon tea and the canal centre is nearby.

None of the Palmerstonian Martello towers of Kent and Sussex were built in West Sussex, but we do have the very first Palmerstonian Fort at Shoreham, built in 1857 against the renewed threat from France, this time by Napoleon III and the **9. Fort at Littlehampton**, which was built three years earlier in 1854. This replaced a gun battery that had been on the east side of the river mouth since 1764. As a prototype for the Palmerstonian forts, it is important as it was experimental and without it, none of the forts that protected Portsmouth or Shoreham Fort would probably have been built. Guns were again in place by 1857 and for thirty years the mouth of the Arun was strongly protected until technical changes rendered it obsolete by 1873. By this time the size and power of naval guns had developed so much that they would have been able to destroy the fort, but nevertheless, like Shoreham Fort it still remained in use until 1906. By 1914 though the Fort was seen as unsuitable for troops and in the Second World War it was unused despite its prime location; the local authorities planning just to block the Arun instead. The area surrounding it was used by an exciting armed force in the Second World War, however, Ian Fleming's Commando unit of 30 AU used to shoot on the beach and were based briefly in the town.

Following the war, the Littlehampton Gazette of 1955 wrote about the delicious tale of a tunnel between the town and the fort and another to the

Pathway by Littlehampton Fort

sea, but this is likely to be unlikely. Since 2011, the team at the fort have worked hard to restore it and protect it from the vegetation that has grown around the site. Thankfully, Littlehampton's sand dunes have drifted up to protect the building and you can now walk among them on rope walkways to tour the site.

Sussex without Satnav: The fort is at (aptly named) Rope Walk and to reach it from the Wey and Arun, take the B2133, A29 and the A284. You then need to go down Ford Road, Ferry Road and finally Rope Walk. From Littlehampton we now go to its sister fort on Shoreham Beach.

10. Shoreham Fort (also known as Kingston or Shoreham Redoubt) is in much better condition than its Littlehampton predecessor and has had a more exciting history. It also benefits from having learnt from the weaknesses of its more westerly sister; providing overhead protection for the garrison inside but still also using new building techniques to cope with rifle fire, such as a Carnot wall. The fort claims to be the last fort to still feature one of these rarities designed to protect rifle-firing infantry.

It may seem strange that such an ancient port as Shoreham only acquired a defensive site in the 1850s, but silt movements leading to the transient nature of the mouth of the Adur meant that the river was changing and only gained its current entrance by 1816. Once the shape of the harbour stabilized then trade moved from Brighton (which was officially a port at this time, despite only having a beach) and needed protection. The construction of the port's piers also helped make the port entrance permanent and so it was decided to construct a building overseeing the comings and goings and to ensure that a French attack on the port, like in 1628, could never happen again. The improvements on Littlehampton and a later midlife rebuild led to Shoreham's fort having a longer shelf life than Littlehampton, with soldiers staying in the fort until 1906 and defences after that. Unlike Littlehampton, it was used in the Second World War, but also it had another role, that as a film studio when Shoreham Beach (or Bungalow Town as it was known) was used for the fledgling British movie industry in the 1910s.

From the madness of war, we move to the war against madness. Victorian West Sussex has a large and very prominent monument to the treatment of

mental health that is worthy of a visit for several reasons. **11. St Francis'**
Hospital, in Haywards Heath. A mile from the main railway, Sussex's
County Lunatic Asylum (which would become St Francis' Hospital)
opened in 1859. The hospital, which once had its own farm, brewery and
bakery, since 1998 has been the Southdown Park housing development but
the yellow and red brick Venetian-style building is still one of the county's
largest and most impressive Victorian developments. The hospital led the
way in treatment of the insane; rejecting chains and straitjackets for pet
therapy, furniture making and joining the hospital's very own band. Its
gardens, spacious landscape and views of the Downs were said to work
wonders. It was said to even be completely self-sufficient except for tea
and sugar.

Sussex without Satnav: From Littlehampton to Worthing take the A259
all the way east into Worthing, you will be pointed down to the seafront
at Goring and then continue east to Grand Avenue. Parking is (at time of
writing) easy and free.

12. The Worthing Metropole, Worthing was once planned so that Worthing
would have its own glamourous Metropole Hotel to rival Brighton's. The
huge hotel seems to be part of a development which commenced in
1893 with what was a presumable first, east-facing wing, built in Grand
Avenue. A further south-facing main wing seems to have been planned
as the development was incomplete at the south end and the first wing
being a less desirable east-facing development when the west of Worthing
was undeveloped as far as Grand Avenue at that time when the seafront
was empty seems bizarre. Planning permission had been granted for 370
beds, which is bigger than the completed wing alone. The Metropole was
designed to complement a planned West Worthing Pier that would be at the
end of Grand Avenue but that also never materialized. There are clues today
of steps on the promenade and the start of a grand entrance. The hotel,
which wasn't part of the same chain that owned Brighton's, London's,
Monte Carlo's and Canne's Metropoles was a similar curvaceous style to
the Metropole at Folkestone decorated with Dutch gables. It was apparently
less than half-built when financial disaster occurred and the hotel remained

a shell for thirty years. A planning application to complete the development with a south-facing wing with three towers and call it a hotel again failed, due to yet another economic depression. It eventually was completed as 'Grand Avenue Mansions' and then 'The Towers' complex of flats, possibly due to the planned towers that had been on the aborted southern wing. This is today known as Dolphin Lodge and the 1960s saw the addition of a completed southern end, in a style very much of that era.

Dolphin Lodge today is worth a visit as a unique Worthing and Sussex building architecturally but also perhaps as Sussex's most unlucky building. It is also an interesting example of a study in what could have been. In some alternate reality there is a bustling Worthing Metropole as the centre of the successful seaside resort of West Worthing, complete with adjacent pier and numerous holidaymakers. Worthing could have even started to rival Brighton as a conference resort, as it would have had a huge luxury hotel with an exclusive name. Sadly, Worthing never achieved the building of a hotel on that scale and the area has ended up, as Antony Edmonds suggests in his *Lost Buildings of Worthing - A Historic Town and Its People* as a 'Bucharest-on-sea'. In one way, at least Dolphin Lodge is an exercise in efficiency. A lot of hotels ended up being converted into flats after a spell as a hotel like Folkestone's Metropole; Worthing's Metropole after a spell as an empty shell went straight to that state and missed out the time as a hotel altogether.

Worthing Metropole

13. The Towers. Travelling east to our final destination in Victorian Sussex, we encounter another set of Towers. The building took its name from them and today The Towers School, (or to give it its full previous name: The Towers - The Convent of the Blessed Sacrament) is a delightfully unusual building for Sussex. It is a gothic crenellated faux-chateau that dominates the village of Upper Beeding. Not many schoolgirls can boast they attend a school in Sussex that is actually also the home of the Sisters of the Blessed Sacrament, or the one-time home of two princesses. Not many schools have a history that starts back in 1670s France either.

Blessed Peter Vigne (1670–1740) was a priest, and later a missionary born in Privas, who in 1712 established the Congregation of the Sisters of the Blessed Sacrament at Boucieu-le-Roi. Nearly two centuries later, in 1903, religious schools in France were being closed down due to anti-religious sentiment in France. Luckily, Maling Wynch, a friend of the Sisters in England and France invited them to take up sanctuary and a new home in Upper Beeding. The unusual buildings they would eventually purchase on the Henfield Road already had near-neighbouring monks further up the road at St Hugh's Charterhouse at Shermanbury. It was originally built by George Smith; partly on the site of an older house, 'Wheelers', which dated from the 1750s and remained sometime after the later house was built in 1883. Perhaps inspired by nearby Castletown, where buildings had existed since at least 1808, Smith's house was built in the style of part-crenellated castle and is an example in Victorian eccentricity and extravagance. The beginnings of the house are as mysterious as its look; Smith was an architect who bought the part-finished house and completed its construction before moving in with his family. It became known locally as 'Smith's Folly' in its early days and was finished in a more economical style than the earliest parts of the building.

Smith's building by 1903 was leased by the brother-in-law of Mrs Maling Wynch, who was a friend of the Congregation and would later join them to become Sister Mary Agnes. The good Sister eventually purchased the building by 1908 from its owner by that time, Arthur Payne, and kindly left it to the Congregation in her will, so that it could continue providing a home for the Sisters and continue teaching the girls who had first joined the school as pupils in 1903. The 80ft-high main tower was lowered to make it safer during the First World War, and the remaining towers were given spires so the building gained a slightly-French look. The hunting lodge, as The Towers had been when leased by Mrs Wynch, then gained a third floor. This was soon needed as the school roll soon grew in number from the original intake of five girls and progressed to even include two princesses. Princess Charlotte of Monaco after her time at the school became mother to Prince Rainier and mother-in-law to the actress Grace Kelly. Even appearing as a boys' private school in the BBC TV series *'Cuffs'*, The Towers today is a unique and romantic-looking place of education and religious contemplation unlike any other.

Sussex without Satnav: Get onto the A27 east out of Worthing until the Shoreham flyover where you come off and take the A283 north towards Henfield. As the Henfield Road turns right, take that towards the Rising Sun roundabout, where you take a right turn briefly along the A2037 road until you see the Towers on your left. Visitors would need to call 01903 817841 to attend a mass or celebrate the Liturgy of the hours in the magnificent chapel. For tours of this unusual and wonderful school, call the school reception on 01903 812185.

The Towers, Beeding, c.1905. Courtesy of Antony Edmonds

CHAPTER 10

Edwardian and First World War Sussex

1. Stansted Park, in the extreme west of the county is one of our few Edwardian houses, built in 1903, although its style belongs to the Christopher Wren era. This is because the house was rebuilt on the 'footprint' of a seventeenth-century house after suffering a disastrous fire in 1900. The previous house dated from 1684 and was 200m to the south-west. It was built by William Talman who also designed Uppark, and its early twentieth century rebuild tried roughly to recreate the design. That replaced a hunting lodge which had stood on the site since the eleventh century until being destroyed in 1644 during the Civil War. Again, like Uppark it enjoys a fine view over the coast, with Chichester Harbour in the distance and can keep all the family happy with a tea room, garden centre, plant shop, yew maze, magnificent walks and miniature railway. All this before you even explore the magnificent Grade II listed house and fifteenth-century chapel.

Stansted Park became home of the Earls of Bessborough in the twilight years of stately houses in 1924, at a time when other families were selling or struggling with their great houses. This was as their seat in Ireland was destroyed by a civil disturbance in those turbulent years there after the Great War. The Earls would not live in the house for long though and in 1983 the 10th Earl donated the house and gardens to a trust which runs it today. It was also the home, like Parham, to evacuees in the Second World War and today is busy with many events and not just children, but their whole families too.

Sussex without Satnav: Stansted Park is nearest to Rowlands Castle. It is possible to bike or walk from there as only about 1.5 miles. By car, if coming from Chichester, take the A27 west and then head north on the

Horndean Road from the A27. You get to Rowlands Castle by a road that becomes Comley Road, Whichers Gate Road and then heads east as Redhill Road after you pass the Staunton Arms. From Rowlands a signposted lane east takes you to Stansted Park.

The peaceful Edwardian Era, the last great era of empire for Britain moved into the woes of the First World War. Despite fears of invasion, and what Brighton's Clock Tower would look like in flames from air raids, Sussex was physically unscathed from enemy fire in the First World War. The same cannot be said for its people, however, with war memorials popping up in every town, city and village across Britain apart from fifty-two (a mere fourteen never lost anyone in both wars). Nowhere in Sussex is called what is known as a 'Thankful village'—somewhere that has never lost anyone in any wars. This suggests the pressure men faced to enlist in the First World War was great, with the action sometimes being audible across the Channel and men travelling to the trenches were constantly in view across the county. This means there should be plenty to see from the Great War, but a century on, this is not the case. It is easier to say where First World War work or action took place than to see where it did. Our imagination and detective powers are often needed just as much to envisage these events of a century ago as for Sussex's Iron or Stone Age sites. Often the main reminder across Sussex of its wartime role are the names on every war memorial in each town and village of the Sussex men who didn't return. Rather than feature any in particular, we return to somewhere we have already featured in chapters on other eras. **2. Chichester Cathedral's St George's Chapel** has the roll of all the names of the Royal Sussex Regiment (RSR) soldiers who died in the conflict so is a good place to take into account the enormity of the scale of the war. It has been the Regiment's memorial ever since 1921 and its 6,800 names of all ranks line the south and west walls. The Regiment restored the chapel when it was created and reinstalled the wall separating it from the rest of the cathedral so those paying their respects have some privacy. You can also find the names of the 1,024 Second World War RSR fallen next to the altar in a memorial book. Should you visit on St George's day then a memorial service in the chapel is aptly held.

The First World War saw the construction of short-lived training airfields on Cobnor Point in Rustington, at Ford Junction and even nearly at Goring (between where Limbrick Lane and Field Place are now) but it is the one that was at **3. Tangmere** which is the only one that has a lively and thriving museum which is well worth a visit. Ford today just has a later jet age aircraft as a gate guardian to the Industrial estate to remind us of its role from the First World War. We think of Tangmere more to do with the Second World War but the airfield was discovered in time to play an important role in the First World War. Like Shoreham, it was discovered by a pilot making a landing and recommending it for use as an airfield, but in Tangmere's case the pilot made a forced landing and then recommended that the land (part of the

CHICHESTER CATHEDRAL, as it would be under GERMAN BOMBARDMENT.

SAVE SUSSEX FROM THIS.
The Mighty German Forces are almost as near Sussex as London is to Brighton.

JOIN THE SOUTHDOWNS
(KITCHENER'S ARMY)
and Shield Sussex from what the Germans are doing to — Belgium and France. —

A propaganda poster suggesting what a bombing raid could be like in Chichester during the Great War

Goodwood Estate) would make a rather good runway. Lieutenant Geoffrey Dorman's forced landing on his way to Gosport led to Tangmere being used by No.1 Squadron, who were the first to be sent to France. Ninety-one, 92 and 93 Squadrons of the RFC (the RAF's the First World War predecessor) then made the airfield their home before the US American Expeditionary Force moved in. An earlier version of the bombing war against Germany in the Second World War would have taken place from both the 200 acres that made up Tangmere and its smaller sibling at Ford with long-range bombers had the Armistice not been signed in November 1918.

Middleton Seaplane Aircraft Works - People not only had to fly aeroplanes; they needed to build them. **4. Middleton Seaplane Aircraft Works** was more substantial and can be tracked down still. Middleton-On-Sea was a site of manufacturing of early aircraft even before the First World War, and so was one of the country's earliest of its kind. The area attracted the engineer

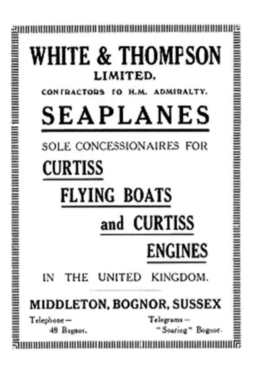

Middleton Aircraft Works advertisement, 1915

Norman Thompson to create the works as early as 1912 due to its sandy beach which could be used as a runway at low tide and windy nature to help with lift. Middleton has had problems with floods and so aptly, the company went from aircraft that took off just on land to also seaplanes by 1913, the decision being helped by Middleton losing some of its sandy beach in a major storm. Not just the sea but work flooded in, as the Norman Thompson Flight Company (as it later became during the First World War) boomed with naval aircraft contracts—even when its major funder, Dr Douglas White left the company to join the Royal Naval Medical Corps in the First World War. Around 250 aircraft were built by the end of the war by its workforce, which, at its peak, between Middleton and Littlehampton weren't far off 1,000 strong—with others employed at Littlehampton making the flying boats hulls.

Thompson had even been joined before the war in his endeavours by Frederick Lanchester, the name behind the famous British early motoring manufacturers (and designer for Daimler) who grew up in Brighton. Thompson and White's efforts in 1915 leave us with perhaps the worst ever nickname for an aircraft—the Bognor Bloater! Ten of these seaplanes were made and the RAF has unsurprisingly, unlike the name 'Typhoon', never brought the name 'Bloater' back. Despite its name, the Bloater was a rather slim aeroplane, probably inspired by the bloater fish, which has a similar shape to the plane's fuselage, (until they are bloated in cooking). The unique monocoque construction of its fuselage, where its copper and mahogany body was covered in a skin, would have looked like it had scales, and when varnished it would have looked shiny like fish skin, hence the name.

Changes to naval requirements and technical difficulties with aircraft led to orders drying up rather than flooding in and the company went into liquidation by July 1919. The aircraft factory, whose land took up 10 acres became part of the 'New City' holiday resort built by Sir Walter Blount, following local residential development by Captain R. Coldicott in 1921. The 'New City' was a prototype for later Butlins-esque developments, but not the site of Butlins today, although it is believed the Butlins site had some links with the Littlehampton wing of the business. New City was very forward-looking for its time in planning for cars to park in the grounds, and then went on to become the Southdean Hotel and Sports Club, Club 18-30, Warner's and finally owned by Shearings before being sold for housing in 1995. In its heyday of the thirties and forties the buildings hosted guests such as Oswald Mosley and the Blackshirts. The former erecting shed became the Pavilion Dance Hall near Waterloo Square in Bognor, which then went on to burn down in 1948. Sadly, the only other remaining building from the site, which became Wilmotts motor garage in Aldwick Road, was demolished in a building development in 2013. This means that there may not be much to remind us of these early figureheads in aviation as you walk along the beach today in Middleton. However, we here in Sussex had not just one of the country's first aircraft factories, but the first to build seaplanes, which then became the site of our first holiday camp, all of which makes Middleton worth an hour or so of your time. If you're still not convinced, then parts of Lanchester's early 'Grey Angel' aircraft are meant to possibly still be underneath Middleton pond, so you might be visiting the resting place of one of Britain's earliest aircraft!

Sussex without Satnav: To get to the site of the former Air Works, Sea Lane is south of the B2132 which runs through Middleton and Elmer. From Middleton to Slindon, take the B2132 north towards the A259. Turning right onto the A259, after a few yards, take the Bilsham Road again north, until you turn left onto the B2233. Head west briefly before heading north again up a longer stretch—along Yapton Lane. This then takes you onto the A27, turn and head west along the A27 until the roundabout with the A29 and head up the A29 until you get to Slindon.

In the early stages of the war, airship technology outstripped that of aeroplanes and Sussex needed airship mooring stations. Sussex was handy for airships for spotting German submarines that were bringing Britain's Merchant Navy to its knees.

5. First World War Airship base at Slindon was built partly as air defences over Sussex and was fortified following an audacious raid by a lone Zeppelin on 25 September 1916. The Zeppelin threat and action had been felt most heavily over East Anglia and London so this was a rarity, the airship in question having flown along the Sussex coast to raid Portsmouth. On its return, Zeppelin L31 was witnessed returning from Midhurst to Steyning. The nearby British Airship base in Slindon allowed Britain to have its own airship presence and three of the gas-filled 'blimps' were based off the main drive to Nore Wood on the Slindon Estate, which today is owned by the National Trust. The 200 acre base had airships made up in Wormwood Scrubs, an area more famous for its prison than its aeronautical expertise and came into their own towards the end of the war, when they had some successes. Bizarrely, it was an outpost for the distant main Polegate air station in East Sussex, and was still in use in the 1930s as an emergency landing station for the air-filled beasts. When mentioning follies in the earlier chapter, we left out the folly at Slindon Estate. This, which looks like a gateway without a building attached, was the destination for morse messages which were sent (and received) from here; perhaps Britain's most bizarre-looking wartime communications centre. The open land where the airships were moored is still open land today and so one of Britain's obsolete wartime locations is also a picturesque walking spot today.

Lunch Locally: Slindon has a good village shop and tea room, just off the A29. It has plenty of National Trust maps of the Slindon Estate to help you locate the former location of the airship base.

6. Worthing Dome - The government in the First World War needed to control minds as well as airspace and our next site to visit is an example of the consequences of the success of the government's anti-German propaganda.

Worthing Dome

The Dome first opened on 15 April 1911, as a multipurpose entertainment facility, which was largely dominated by roller skating (the centre even had its own roller skating team). The building was completed on 7 October 1911 with the front section opened and the dome completed, at which point a cinema screen was opened upstairs (the current Screen 2 sits partly on that site). It's believed that between £5,000–£6,000 was spent on the building. It was originally named The Kursaal, named after similar sites across Europe that Swiss-born owner Carl Seebold had seen (he had worked at one in Southend before moving to Worthing). In 1915, the building was renamed due to anti-German sentiment over the First World War. A competition was run in the local paper, and the prize of £1 was offered. The name tended to be used in Switzerland, not Germany, and meant 'cure hall', so the name change was technically pointless, but another example of the de-Germanization of business and organization names at this time. Even the Germanic 'dachshund' was changed to 'sausage dog' after some of these dogs had been stoned by thuggish so-called patriots.

The building also witnessed a meeting in 1913 of a group who were also to be affected by the demands of the war. The Suffragettes held a rally which drew large numbers but also anti-suffrage sentiment from locals and a swift exit was needed using rear doors. The Suffragettes would relinquish their militant campaign of activities to get the vote during the war to focus on serving the Home Front. Ironically, this wartime change probably helped them get suffrage more than their militant actions had. Due to the growing popularity of cinema, the building was swapped over in 1921, so that the downstairs was converted into a cinema and upstairs became a ballroom. The current interior of the cinema is largely the same as it was in 1921, so a trip to the Dome is today a trip back in time to the era just after the First World War and to a building never the same due to the Great War.

Sussex without Satnav: From Slindon, return south back down the A29 and turn east at the roundabout that joins the A27 to Worthing. As before, from the A27 you can easily find your way to Worthing Seafront. The Dome at Worthing is on the A259 which is the coast road at this point and you continue east on this to Shoreham. To Buckingham Park or Slonk Hill you need to head up inland to the Old Shoreham Road by taking the first left at the Ropetackle Roundabout, which has the Bridge Inn on it.

The military population of Sussex grew as huge temporary training camps in **7. Shoreham and Roffey near Horsham** sprung up. Despite the fact they became almost small towns there is little to point us to their whereabouts today. Shoreham was the most impressive and was the focus of an exhibition about it back in 2014. It grew up on the downs above Buckingham Park and on Slonk Hill, itself possibly supposedly no stranger to soldiers as it is believed to be a Saxon battle site as mentioned earlier. Even Buckingham Park itself ended up being dug up to support the camp in places, and the local community were engaged too, providing extra lodging when needed and doing laundry. Mock battles took place on the Downs due to the Shoreham camp as trench systems were recreated to aid training. The Downs also made life in the camp more difficult also when a landslide of mud poured through the camp.

8. Shoreham Airport was another airfield that some of the Royal Flying Corps (predecessor of the RAF) embarked from for France in 1914, not all of which completed the journey. Some were reputedly have said to have ended up flying backwards when windspeeds proved to be stronger than the horsepower of the engines. Shoreham was also expected to defend London from the threat from Germany—with one bomber! The terrible events of the Shoreham Airshow disaster of 2015 must never be forgotten, but we must also remember Shoreham's long and illustrious past as a military airbase in both world wars and as a civilian airport too. Shoreham has also had an accident before at its air show and in the First World War there was even a crash near the former Sussex Pad pub, similar to the site of the 2015 crash. It has this long heritage as it is one of the earliest centres of aviation in the world; continually in use since 1910. It is even the location of the first recorded cargo flight (a box of light bulbs). The famous Cecil and Eric Pashley (still commemorated at the airport) moved their flying club from Brooklands to Shoreham in 1913, but then left it behind in 1914 as they moved into war service. The airport then became an important training centre in the First World War, even claiming to be there at the very start of the Canadian Air Force.

After the Great War the airfield's future looked in doubt until Cecil Pashley returned to set up the Gnat Aero Company, as well as offering flying tuition and pleasure flights. The interwar years would see the launch of the first aircraft designed in the grounds of the airfield. The thirties saw Shoreham go from strength to strength with its first royal landing, with the Prince of Wales (the future Edward VIII) making a visit, increasing numbers of aero clubs and even an Airshow. Shoreham also got its (now Grade II) art deco Terminal Building in 1935 which is the jewel in the airport's crown today and has been used in a range of TV programmes ever since, including *Poirot*, Helen Mirren's *The Woman In Gold* and the 2005 film *The Da Vinci Code*. In 1936 it was officially opened as Brighton, Worthing and Shoreham Municipal Airport. Shoreham Airport is today very worthy of a visit and a place children or grandchildren will love. The wonderful art deco building

Shoreham Airport

has not just the most exciting and active view of any restaurant and bar in the country, but also a whispering gallery upstairs. This historic and scenic centre of aviation is also the oldest licensed airfield in Britain.

9. Mouse Lane, Steyning - Further inland from Shoreham is an unusual First World War Sussex feature, in that it is a First World War poem recorded in stone in a country lane. The story behind the poem, which you read in Mouse Lane as you walk from Steyning to Chanctonbury Ring, is even more unusual.

Lieutenant John Stanley Purvis (who chose to be called Philip) was not a Sussex man, and there is no clear evidence of him ever having visited the area, but his mysterious and emotive poem *From Steyning to the Ring* (or *Chance Memory* / *The Steyning Poem* as it was originally known) is the most famous literary link to the war of this part of Sussex. It gives Purvis' imaginary account of a soldier in the midst of the horrors of trench warfare about to go over the top and advance. The soldier is clearly missing his life back at home and taking solace from his memories of the track from Mouse Lane to Chanctonbury. However, Steyning Museum reveals not only the full story behind the poem, but that it was released under the pseudonym Philip Johnson, and also originally ended with the line 'I can't forget the narrow lane to Chanctonbury Ring'.

Purvis' journey to Chanctonbury Ring would have been via Steyning Station at that time, as it would have been possible to catch a train from Cranleigh (where he was at that time a teacher and about to depart to serve in the trenches) to Steyning and walk from there through the High Street to Chanctonbury.

On reading the poem below, it is still today hard to imagine that it wasn't written by a serving officer in France but penned instead by an imaginative, and presumably very scared, young man still at school in Cranleigh. Purvis did serve in the trenches, although his brother was killed in 1917, but he didn't leave school until Christmas 1915. It is useful as it tells us that despite increasing censorship by 1915, the horrific conditions in the trenches; the very real chance of death and the fear of the Tommy in the trench had become well known back in Britain, if not ever truly understood by those who hadn't been there. A walk up Mouse Lane is a must for those interested in the First World War in not just Sussex but Britain, as the description by Purvis paints such a terrifying picture. The fear Purvis was facing, or imagining, shows why recruitment decreased in 1915, and why the government subsequently increased the pressure to enlist through propaganda. It tells why conscription, forcing men into the trenches, came in soon after.

I can't forget the lane that goes from Steyning to the Ring
In summer time, and on the Down how larks and linnets sing

High in the sun. The wind comes off the
sea, and Oh the air!
I never knew till now that life in old days was so fair.
But now I know it in this filthy rat infested ditch
When every shell may spare or kill – and God alone knows which.
And I am made a beast of prey, and this trench is my lair.
My God! I never knew till now that those days were so fair.
So we assault in half an hour, and, – it's a silly thing –
I can't forget the narrow lane to Chanctonbury Ring.

Purvis went back to his school at Cranleigh to teach; leaving in 1933 to join the church where he rose to become Canon of York Minster, dying after a long life in 1968. He has left behind many poems but his most mysterious is not only preserved in Mouse Lane, but the original was luckily donated to the very wonderful Steyning Museum; itself well worth a visit.

Sussex without Satnav / Lunch Locally: Take the A283 north out of Shoreham to Steyning (there is a prettier, but windy lane east of Lancing College, but it's single-lane in places and not for those frightened of 4x4s rearing up at them on tight bends). The A283 turns left to Steyning just before Upper Beeding and it's best to follow the Steyning bypass past the town and enter at the Sports Centre entrance to the town, rather than take the first route through the town. Mouse Lane is as the road through Steyning takes a sharp left turn just before the (much recommended) Model Bakery and if you reach the (also recommended) Star Inn then you've gone too far. You're probably best getting a blue parking pass from the Leisure Centre just up the road and leaving the car there as there's no parking in Mouse Lane. It does, however, have Steyning Brewery up it as you approach Purvis' poem carved in stone.

Purvis' poem records the fear of the trenches and the terror those serving in them endured. It is to the east of the county, near to the border with East Sussex that an event took place that ended the ordeal of trench life. It was here in Sussex that the decision was taken to formally end the war. Danny House in Hurstpierpoint does not welcome the public generally as it is a private retirement today but in its main hall is the site of a meeting of the Imperial War Cabinet on 13 October 1918. The terms of the Armistice were agreed here and then cabled to Woodrow Wilson. In the hall at that time were the three future Prime Ministers; Bonar Law, Balfour and Churchill, and the current one, Lloyd George, who was apparently ill in the White Bedroom. He was still able to sign off the Armistice terms though and so not just Sussex men and women but a Sussex house that had been loaned to Lord Riddell for use by Lloyd George and his cabinet was also able to play a role in the war effort.

CHAPTER 11

Interwar, Art Deco/Modernist & Second World War Sussex

Although we have already mentioned it once, to be strictly accurate, it is the interwar period that gives us Shoreham Airport's most famous building, its Terminal Building, and so the fan of art deco buildings needs to use this as their excuse to visit this wonderful site and lunch in the Hummingbird Restaurant there. For an example of rare modernist architecture of the 1930s visit Berthold-Lubetkin housing in Haywards Heath. There is Sea Lane House in East Preston, the only house in Britain wholly designed by the great Bauhaus-trained architect and designer Marcel Breuer, which is Grade II listed as it's one of the most distinguished examples of early twentieth century architecture on the South Coast. Unfortunately, the six-bedroom house built in 1936 is in one of East Preston's two private estates with no through road, so we cannot recommend a visit, unless it's a virtual one online.

In which case, an unusual case of architecture you can see from the era of depression and rearmament is **1. Worthing Town Hall**. Worthing's councillors (first called commissioners) originally met upstairs in the Nelson and then in the Royal Oak and George pubs in Worthing's lost Market Street. Finally, Worthing's first town hall was completed by 1835. This was funded by public subscription and was only meant to be a clock tower, which did arrive but on the top of the town hall the whip-round also paid for. By the 1930s however, it was too small for civic business and pride and was no longer seen to reflect the scale of the growing town of Worthing. It was left to decline and was sadly demolished in 1966 replaced by a set of steps to the hideous 1970s Guildbourne Centre and, ironically, a rather spindly clock tower in a flower bed. Worthing's 1933 town hall building had no fears of being seen as too small; quite the opposite. In a time of depression, locals balked at the scale of the building and its design. Ninety per cent of the workforce were made up of the many unemployed at that time however. The design today doesn't look like a typical 1930s building, with its faux-Georgian appearance. It is a marvellous building inside and out, with the main council chamber and mayor's parlour worth a visit whenever a tour is arranged. The town's Latin motto, which translates as 'from the land fullness and from the sea health', proudly displays across its classical front, with its pediment and clock tower giving it the look of the town hall that Doc Brown hangs off in *Back to the Future*.

Chichester's County Hall has some similarities but although started before the war, was only finished after it, so we will ignore it here.

2. Worthing Pier also has fine examples of 1930s architecture. The Southern Pavilion of Worthing Pier is particularly worthy of a visit.

Depression was one of the causes of the Second World War and the unemployed of the thirties were soon called up to fight or were involved in the construction of military building projects. At the far south-west of

Worthing Pier

the county, Chichester Harbour was soon protected by seaborne invasion and its proximity to the Continent meant it would be useful to both our navy and air force. RAF Thorney was built on Thorney Island in 1938, and was used by both the RAF and FAA (Fleet Air Arm of the Royal Navy) during the Second World War. Coastal defences were built in the harbour, which witnessed at least thirty-two aircraft crash down; thirteen of them in 1940 alone. It was **3. Royal Naval Air Station Ford** that became Sussex's worst-attacked RAF station during the Battle of Britain, with twenty-two dead in the raid on Sunday, 18 August 1940. Ford was also used by both RAF and FAA but was only a training airfield. This made no difference to the Luftwaffe or their information was incorrect as it received the same treatment as other airfields and was attacked by JU87 Stuka dive-bombers. One anti-aircraft gunner was believed decapitated when his head was found on top of sand ruptured from sandbags, but it turned out he'd been buried in the sand, face up from the blast and had the lesser injury of shrapnel cuts instead. Four thousand gallons of fuel burnt viciously after the attack, five aircraft were destroyed and twenty-six damaged. The memorial to the brave staff of Ford is now down the road at Clymping Church with a solitary gate guard aircraft at the entrance to the industrial estate where car boot sales now take place. Ford Open Prison also partially covers the site of this Second World War tragedy. The Royal Navy gave up Ford after the attack and it became an RAF station. It is to the RAF we focus now.

The most glamorous use for a Second World War RAF base must be Westhampnett, which is of course Goodwood today. Perhaps the bravest story of any member of personnel from the services in the Second World War Sussex is of a determined RAF operative during a further Battle of Britain attack. This took place just up the road from Ford at the RAF Radar Station at **4. Poling**. Poling was where WAAF Corporal Avis J. Hearn also faced the might of the Luftwaffe on 18 August but the difference was she was a RDF (as it was called then) aircraft plotter, feeding vital information to the RAF HQ at Stanmore House about where and when the next attack was coming from. Without her, raids could get through and more damage would be done to other RAF stations. Her job saved lives. The other difference was she had a hugely thick concrete roof above her which, if it fell on the Corporal, would have certainly crushed her in an instant.

The final difference about one of the raids Hearn plotted was that it was diving down on the very place she worked, and despite this knowledge she discovered, she refused to leave her post.

Bombs raining down on her failed to budge her from her post, as did the knowledge she was about to face them. The plucky 4ft10 Corporal was told by Stanmore: 'Poling, do you realize the last plot we've been given by you is right above you?' By the time she replied, Stukas were diving down and dropping their fatal cargo all around her. Stanmore heard the explosions down the phone line. Her reply is simply one that should be quoted every year on Sussex Day, as one that certainly sums up the county motto of 'We won't be druv'. Hearn replied: 'The course of the enemy bombers is only too apparent to me because the bombs are almost dropping on my head.'

If the Luftwaffe couldn't move her, her own side had even less luck. Even her Sergeant ordering her to leave her post and take cover was met with refusal. 'I can't', Hearn replied, 'I've got too much information coming through' and she carried on at her post sending through information about every squadron intruding into British airspace. Even when the bombs landed so close they blew out the windows of her building, Avis stayed put, and the operator in Middlesex at Stanmore asked her down the phone after hearing the attack, 'Are you ok, Poling?' Thankfully Avis Hearn was and stayed put for another further twenty minutes until she could do no more as the bombs had severed the phone lines. Then and only then did she take shelter as there was nothing else she could do that day to protect her country. The gap in the RAF's eyes and ears, Radar (as we now call it), was soon plugged with a replacement RDF station at Angmering, so the German raid had only temporary effect. Corporal Hearn went on to receive one of the country's highest awards for bravery, the Military Medal in 1941, and the attack apparently inspired the Radar station attack scene in the 1968 film, *The Battle of Britain*, although its location and outcome changed.

Avis Jean Hearn died in 2008. She deserves to be taught in schools and to be more widely remembered. The building she bravely stayed put in at Poling was later changed into workshops and garages after the station closed in 1956 and is today private housing, which it has been converted into since the 1990s. It is a shame that there is not a memorial to this amazing lady, without whom many more fighters and bombers attacking Britain would have got through on what was called the RAF's 'Hardest Day'.

Ford faced the worst attack in the Second World War but **5. RAF Tangmere** is Sussex's most famous airbase from the Second World War however. With its superb museum, it is one of the sites of the Second World War in Sussex most worth a visit. Its significance in the Second World War also truly make it one of the few places in Britain that helped change the course of the war. RAF airfields like Tangmere were our front line when the Wehrmacht and Luftwaffe reached the coast of France. Like the other airfields in Sector 11 (the South East of England) it would have been all too easy to abandon these airbases when they received the pounding they did from German bombing raids in August and September 1940. Although it was close Fighter Command never pulled their Spitfires and Hurricanes back north of the Thames, so Germany never gained air superiority, which would have been the necessary first step to landing an invasion force across the Channel.

Tangmere is also worthy due not just to its role and the punishment it took, but because of those who served there. Any place that once had the legendary legless pilot Douglas Bader fly from it and H.E. Bates write in whilst stationed there must be worth a few hours of anyone's time. 601 Squadron, based at Tangmere during the Battle of Britain, are also one of the war's more famous squadrons and were known as the 'Millionaire's Squadron' due to their privileged backgrounds. The starting price to enter a game of poker in the squadron mess was apparently £100. Their money apparently didn't help the quality of their radio equipment, however, as on a sortie during the Battle over West Sussex their Commanding Officer was given the codename 'bosom' over his cockpit radio as their target to defend. He misheard the radio message and thought he had to defend the Bosham Inn! This must be the only time in history that an entire RAF squadron of Hurricane fighter aircraft were and gave protection to a pub.

The squadron included the first American pilot to serve in the RAF, William Fiske. Billy Fiske was an RAF pilot who was killed in action in 1940 whilst stationed at Tangmere Aerodrome during the Battle of Britain. Being a Battle of Britain pilot; one of the 'few' alone makes the pilot special, but he was the first American serviceman to serve in the RAF in the

Second World War and the first American serviceman to die in the whole of the six-year conflict. The American, who was born in Chicago in June 1911, is buried in the south-east part of the churchyard of Boxgrove Priory. His funeral was broadcast to the US via Pathe News and can still be viewed today on Pathe's website, where you can see his coffin, draped with both Union Flag and Stars and Stripes being carried towards the church. Billy was already famous before his wartime service, having been also a 1928 and 1932 Olympic champion bobsled driver. Billy died after successfully landing his damaged Hurricane fighter only to be strafed in the cockpit by the Luftwaffe's fighters as they attacked Tangmere. The only remaining part of this station, that was Billy Fiske's last home, is the ailing Air Control Tower, which is in a bad way today. Although the Battle of Britain aircraft tower was demolished, the remaining one built in 1944 would have seen raids to France take off under its direction and played a key role in Britain's high-speed record holding post-war. This important building certainly demands restoration as an example of air control towers of 1940 and a reminder of a key part of the events of that baking-hot summer where a few men ensured Britain stayed in the war and would help bring about war's end in 1945.

Tangmere was also involved in the clandestine Special Operations Executive (SOE) 'Black Lysander' operations where SOE agents were secretly flown in and out of occupied France. Violette Szabo left from Tangmere and was the only woman to receive the George Cross for outstanding service—on her mission from the RAF station. Szabo had a film made about her, directed by Lewis Gilbert: the 1958 film *Carve Her Name With Pride*, starring Virginia McKenna.

Even more famous than Billy Fiske and Violette Szabo, Douglas Bader, the famous legless pilot of the Second World War served at Tangmere. Bader also had a film made about his career by Lewis Gilbert: *Reach For The Sky* in 1956, the title now more famous as the catchphrase of Woody from *Toy Story*. Bader survived, losing both his legs in an air crash in 1931 and eventually badgered the RAF to let him return to duty. He soon made his way up the ranks and was a key supporter of Air Vice-Marshal Sir Keith Park. Park was the proponent of the tactic of using 'Big Wings', where time was taken to amass squadrons in the air under one commander, and

Tangmere

the commander would be Bader. Bader was given the choice of where to fly his 'Big Wings' of multiple squadrons from to attack France, once the defensive strategy of the Battle of Britain in 1940 gave way to going on the offensive in 1941. Bader chose Tangmere, and so should you for a visit. Tangmere is one of the places everyone in or visiting Sussex should know.

Sussex without satnav: There are two ways to Tangmere from the A27—if you're heading from the east, then come off at the Tangmere roundabout and follow the signs to the museum. If you're heading from the west on the A27, cross over and head towards Tangmere at the traffic lights at the junction with Oving. You'll need to be in the right-hand lane.

Someone we associate more with the Cold War, Ian Fleming, spent his war career with the navy and the group of commandos he commanded are said to have provided the inspiration in many ways for the character of Bond. Their special missions in the Second World War certainly include tasks among the Bondesque and their actions seem similar too. Before D-Day, 30 AU were briefly based at Littlehampton. This group, which was recovering from many missions abroad, seemed to enjoy their time in the town and used Littlehampton Beach for target shooting. There is nothing much to see of their time in Sussex but further east, just west of Storrington, is a unique reminder of other rehearsals for D-Day. Up on **6. Kithurst Hill**, a bullet-riddled Mk II Churchill tank is just 500m south-east of the car park on top of the hill—following a pathway through a field and then turn right at the end. The hill can be driven up to from the B2139 Storrington-Amberley road north of the Downs when you turn off at Springhead Farm. It is a bumpy track, however, so a 4x4 is recommended or don't take your brand-new car. The path that goes past the field with the tank is part of the South Downs Way so can be part of your plans whether on foot or in the car. Although parts of the tank were removed for the Bovington Tank Museum down in Dorset, the carcass is still intact and peppered with the impact of dozens of armour-piercing bullets from its days as target practice for Canadians readying themselves for the ill-fated Dieppe raid. Rapid technological advancement meant only the latest marks of tanks were used so this little fella, as a type mostly used for training, wasn't deemed as needed for the Dieppe Raid of 1942. Technological gremlins that had beset this tank also explained why it never had a chance to fight its German counterparts the other side of the Continent.

After the war, civilians would be allowed to reclaim the Downs once more as they stopped being a place for training, so it was vital the detritus of war was cleared. Coastal tank traps were demolished and destroyed from Sussex seafronts at places like Worthing at great effort. Lancing Green simply turned theirs into landscape features that are still there today by burying them. The Churchill that had been used as a dartboard by Canadians was ungraciously pushed into a shell crater and unceremoniously buried, where it remained for half a century. Washington roundabout is still believed to have a tank buried deep beneath the busy road junction today. The Kithurst tank was easier to rediscover though and in 1993 engineers from the army uncovered and removed it into the field next to the crater. Its fifty years' enjoying a subterranean lifestyle have meant it has been less battered by the elements than you would expect a tank of this age to have been and despite its experience at the end of armour-piercing bullets, it is remarkably intact. It cannot be long before it is deemed that we in the twenty-first century decide to do what the soft soil and lofty location deterred our post-war ancestors from and remove this relic from its hilltop graveyard to some worthy museum. Until then, find and consider this rare Second World War artefact—a Canadian training tank that in its working days most likely had brave Canadian tank crew inside from the 14th Canadian Tank Battalion. Some of them would likely have perished trying to gain our first northern foothold on Nazi-occupied Europe.

Further east, we return to one last West Sussex airfield. **7. Shoreham -** came back into importance in the Second World War again. The airport wasn't to experience a peacetime role for long, however, as two years before the Second World War broke out it was used for training RAF volunteers and by the time of the last pre-war air show in 1939 one of the RAF's types of latest fighters, the Hawker Hurricane, were camouflaged and ready for battle. Again, aircraft heading for battle in France headed across the channel from Shoreham. The airport also took on civilian duties simultaneously as it dealt with Croydon Airport's traffic, which had been

Shoreham Airport

rerouted. As the war stopped being phoney, it seriously looked like the airport could become one of the Nazis' objectives should invasion succeed. Thanks to the RAF's successes in the Battle of Britain this never occurred but damaged Spitfires and Hurricanes used Shoreham to land at, as did even one German fighter! Blenheim and Beaufighter aircraft were stationed here, as was even one flight of Hurricanes. The rest of the war saw the airfield serve in an air-sea rescue role, where it had Spitfires and other aircraft operate from Shoreham (and saving 598 lives) before assisting the Free French Air Force on D-Day.

North of Shoreham, two statues which miraculously survived being in the heart of the London Blitz are today at The Towers School in Upper Beeding. The Towers had a fellow convent at Brompton Square in London, which in September 1940 was hit by a bomb creating a 35ft deep and 27ft wide crater; destroying its chapel. Despite the destruction, a statue of St Joseph was unharmed despite teetering on the edge of the crater. Another statue, of Our Lady, was blasted clear of the chapel and to the end of the convent's gardens; only losing one finger in the process. The Convent's nuns although thankfully survived the direct hit on their London home, moved to much safer locations, including Upper Beeding afterwards where they served the convent here and the school's girls for their remaining years. The statues came with them and one can still be seen in the gardens of The Towers today.

CHAPTER 12

Post- and Cold War Sussex

As the Second World War transformed into the Cold War, Sussex needed homes, not great architecture, and so we have little of exception to note. Crawley and other new towns may one day merit historical tours but for now they are too recent to seem from the distant past. Concrete and glass replaced intricate detail and so our buildings from that era still seem harsh, brutal and unforgiving. This is reflected in the comparative lack of listing of buildings or visitor sites of note that can inspire and provoke awe. Many of these, such as the Festival Theatre at Chichester, still divide opinion. One building of note though is Chichester's Library in Tower Street. This circular building was the first to offer a fully computerized issuing system, the first in the country and its books were catalogued by computer as early as 1974. Its unusual design means that today it is Grade II listed.

As the Cold War emerged and the threat from Germany faded, Sussex was less important strategically as it wasn't the most direct route for the new Soviet threat. It would be the east of the country that was now the front line for British airbases. This didn't stop Sussex still being touched by the Cold War, especially in its early years as the threat from the USSR emerged and the spectre of nuclear war became a possibility. Our Second World War airfields became prisons, housing estates, farmland once more or civilian airfields such as Goodwood and Shoreham.

1. English Martyrs Catholic Church, Goring, is a 1960s church but with a replica inside of the ceiling of the Sistine Chapel (the only one in the world). It took five and a half years for parishioner Gary Bevans to produce between 1987–1993 at two thirds of the scale of the actual ceiling. It is very unusual and an unexpected visitor hotspot.

Above, below and overleaf: *English Martyrs Catholic Church*

2. Tangmere's time was not yet up as an airbase though and this historic airbase, which had started its life in 1916, would still remain a part of Britain's defences until 1970. More importantly, it would be the launch pad of some of the world's latest and fastest aircraft. Furthermore, it also was a place that made history, as the airbase that the world's actual fastest aircraft flew from, zooming between Worthing and Littlehampton, not just once, but twice in 1946 and 1953. Thanks to Tangmere, Sussex was the place to the see the world's fast-moving flying manned object.

This is because after the war the airfield was home to the RAF's High Speed Flight, and the world airspeed record was broken here in September 1946 and August 1953. The field was also modified for use by Meteor jet fighters in the 1950s. The base closed in 1970 although the airfield continued to be used by a gliding school until 1975. In 1982 a museum was founded by volunteers to tell the story of the airfield and the Tangmere Military Aviation Museum, as it is known, is currently located on the edge of the former airfield. Today Tangmere is a suburb of Chichester, the airfield encroached upon by housing and industry, but a stretch of runway remains and in that one corner the museum to enthral all ages, complete with models, uniforms, actual aircraft and simulators, staffed by volunteers whose passion for the place is clear to see. This is probably as the museum's volunteers are many ex-RAF personnel. Not many museums can tell the story of an RAF airfield from 1916 to the nuclear age. Tangmere is a place of Britain reaching its post-war limits, before our slide from being amongst the world's leading technical powers. It also tells the tale of this one-time outpost of democracy in that balmy hot summer of dogfights and death, and of the RAF's battle to stop Hitler's winning spree continuing across the Channel. The museum is still undertaking many restorations of Cold War aircraft too and it is a great morning or afternoon out for a trip about different generations of history that can bring the generation in your family together.

Sussex is lucky to have a second military aviation museum, at the north of the county. Although it is not technically in Sussex, it is only just over the border and includes the story of one of our airports so qualifies sneakily on this account. Charlwood was once in Sussex, and as this is Visitors' *Historic* Britain, the past is key here!

Sussex without Satnav: Take the A27 east from Tangmere until you reach the A23 north of Brighton. Follow the A23 north to Gatwick and once at Gatwick, follow the signs to Charlwood and you will reach...

Meteor under restoration at Tangmere

3. Gatwick Aviation Museum which now opens Fridays to Sundays and has benefitted from a recent revamp with great new hangers. It even starts up Cold War aircraft, such as their Shackleton and English Electric Lightning so you can hear their engines roar and spit. Being near Gatwick Airport has a clear advantage here!

Far less known than Tangmere, as it was very much an amateur operation until recently, 'GAM' has recently increased its opening hours, professionalized its set-up and deserves much wider publicity than it has had to date. It focuses just on the post- and early to mid-Cold War era, which it refers to as the 'Golden Age of British aviation'. It certainly does make the visitor yearn for the days when we had our own aircraft companies and were able to build our own military aircraft without partnership. It has come a long way from the early 1980s when it was Orchard Farm, an intensively-reared battery hen operation. One hundred and fifty thousand cramped eye-laying birds have now been replaced by ten metal birds who were once used to the skies, and their recent move indoors has meant increased maintenance and restoration can continue. This means the museum is hoping to prolong the life of these Cold War winged wonders but also have more of their engines up and running on a regular basis. Although recent legislation means families are not able to get inside the cockpits of the aircraft, the one exception is the Avro Shackleton, younger cousin of the Lancaster, which was still in use in the RAF up until the early 1990s.

Gatwick Aviation Museum is here today despite the odds due to the little-known story of local businessman Peter Vallance who started off the museum from his private collection in 1987. Vallance, who sadly died during a heart operation in 2013, seems to have spent most of the last two and a half decades of his life battling Mole Valley Council in Surrey who seemed for a long while to come up with every argument possible not to have a museum with aircraft right next to… Gatwick Airport, which has apparently the odd aircraft or two in it if my sources are correct! Vallance invested all his assets into making the museum work and even wisely set up for the museum to be turned into a charitable trust in the event of his demise. This is how it operates today. Vallance's years of struggle with bureaucrats in the courts of the land mean today we thankfully have a museum solely dedicated to the Cold War's airborne warriors and illustrious names such as Avro, Hawker, Gloster, De Havilland, English Electric, Blackburn, and Percival are still preserved, and not just in history books. Vallance's actions do make us wonder whether perhaps if the museum had been a few hundred yards away here in Sussex, or Charlwood was still in this county (as it once was) things might have been easier?

Tangmere and GAM tell of the aircraft that protected us in the Cold War but if aircraft such as the Shackleton would only have warned us about attacks, not prevented the successful missile strikes from the Soviet Union. Sussex has a range of reminders that the county was ready to try and survive nuclear Armageddon, and, bizarrely it seems now, observe and report as nuclear bombs rained down. With the depressing thought that nuclear watchposts were once needed, we venture east from Gatwick to Cuckfield to an example of a Cold War bunker that can be visited.

Sussex without Satnav: From Charlwood, take Ifield Road, Charlwood Road and Ifield Avenue to Crawley Avenue and the A23—head south until the B2115 exit off the A23 to Warninglid and Cuckfield Village. Now take Slough Green Lane and then the B2115, B2114 and B2036 to Newbury Lane.

4. Cuckfield Royal Observer Corps Bunker, like the one in Lancing, was one of an incredible 1563 ROC bunkers that were dug out after the Second World War, but unlike Lancing it occasionally opens for visitors to explore its subterranean depths and relive the Cold War's darkest potential days. Cuckfield Museum has helped organize visits in the past of the bunker, built in 1962 at the height of the Cold War with the Cuban Missile Crisis reaching its peak. Not until 1991 was the bunker finally closed and it has been restored as a museum to its early 1990s appearance, with the appropriate equipment, rations and paperwork. The bunkers were dug following a 1955 order that the ROC were not just to observe and warn about future attacks, but to measure their intensity and damage caused. A number of the sites were where Second World War observation sites had been, but the difference was these would be at least 15ft below ground and would be staffed by scientific offers with resources to measure any blast and its damage caused. The thing that grabs you most about these bunkers of course is that these men who staffed them knew that if they were ever ordered to enter them for real, they would have to say goodbye to their families, enter these bunkers and witness their families probably perish. They would have survived any initial blasts but would have re-entered a world some weeks later that would be so toxic their deaths would have come not that much later, but would have been one of a painful, radiation-infused demise, with food supplies and water toxic.

The bunkers were vital though, with their role being to also enable emergency authorities to decide which services could remain in operation, and where to direct precious resources and manpower. They would also advise local populations on when to seek shelter, by sounding the famous four-minute warning. Sussex's shelters for the VIPs and members of regional government were larger and more substantial, but we will have to wait for *Visitors' Historic Britain: East Sussex* for a look at a local one in Lewes. Cuckfield gives us an interesting view into this most horrific of alternative realities and with many of these bunkers being flooded, reused by telecoms companies, bought by individuals, having collapsed or been vandalized, we should thank the volunteers who run these open days in the bunker. They bring this most frightening part of the Cold War so vividly to life once more. For open days, see the Cuckfield bunker's Facebook page—the bunker is just off Newbury Lane in the village. The last open day each year is usually early in August and one this year saw a visitor from as far afield as Alaska! The bunker's saviours were not your most predictable of restorers either, which makes it more interesting. Ed Coombes, from Sayers Common, had been a cardiology nurse and Mark Russell was a mortgage consultant, but the latter was a member of ROC Remembered organization. Cuckfield's bunker is all the more unique in the county as Southwick's has been filled in with concrete and Horsham's, which closed in 1968, although in good condition when last opened has no plans to allow access. Hopefully Horsham's bunker will enjoy the same fate as this wonderful Cold War reminder.

Sussex without Satnav: Retrace the last directions to the A23 and head south to Brighton, turning onto the A27 east towards the Shoreham Flyover, turning south off it before it crosses the Adur. At the roundabout at the bottom, take the Shoreham turnoff and at the Amsterdam pub turn left along the Old Shoreham Road. From this road, turn left when you see the sign for Mill Hill. When parked up on Mill Hill, you can walk to Truleigh Hill.

5. RAF Truleigh Hill, on top of the Downs above Shoreham, was first built as a Radar station in 1939 but following the escalation of Cold War tensions, a bunker complex was built below the surface and the capability of the station, which had been designed to spot low-flying aircraft, was upgraded. It only existed for six years before being decommissioned in 1958 and although the bunker is today unused, the surface communications site is used by the emergency services. What is remarkable though about Truleigh Hill is not just the bunker complex still there under this peak of the Downs, but the fact the guardhouse to the complex was designed in the style of a brick-built farmhouse with verandah so that potential attackers would be misled—a theory ruined somewhat by up to six pylons being stationed in the 'farm's' vicinity. It is such a shame that this complex, similar to the Beachy Head one that will be featured in *Visitors' Historic Britain: East Sussex* is not open to the public and the site is secure. Nevertheless, a walk up to Truleigh Hill is always worth the views you get from the Downland peak, but also to walk where those involved in the Cold War once beavered away below ground.

Sussex without satnav: Retrace your steps but westwards this time along the Old Shoreham Road. When you get back to the Amsterdam, head south (turning left) to the Bridge Inn and then take the A259 coast road east to Brooklands Park, which has car parks to its north and west. The west is closest to the site of the bunker—just above the children's paddling pool at Brooklands on the very informal golf course and park there. Brooklands is free to enter (you just pay for the parking) and is a good family location. It also has the mouth of the Teville stream which was once navigable up to Broadwater, and so would have been Worthing Harbour, had Worthing been of any size in the Middle Ages.

6. Lancing was the site of another ROC bunker that would have observed the demise of Worthing's population from Brooklands Park. Although the

ROC site, Lancing.

bunker has long been closed and covered over, being in a park (strangely juxtaposed just above a children's paddling pool) means you can walk where ROC volunteers would have been stationed deep below as the bomb dropped.

The nuclear side of the Cold War still manages to send chills up our spines today with how near we came to Armageddon at times, especially at the time of writing when we have the particular American president we do at the moment. So, let us finish this book with the wish that by the time the sequel to this book on East Sussex comes out, we have a calmer world situation and better candidates for world leadership. Of course, if this was the movies, we always have our favourite spy to keep us safe no matter what; born of the Cold War, James Bond is the Cold War character who refuses to die and has survived into the post-Cold War age. Perhaps it is fitting then that we finish this final chapter and the book itself with the

Cold War's greatest spy—even if he is just fictional. **6. Amberley Museum** is not just one of West Sussex's greatest days out for all the family. It is not just a great place for visitors who love the historic side of Britain, and especially one that tells the tale of much that is wonderful about West Sussex. It also was the film setting for the last of the Roger Moore Bond films in 1985, *A View To A Kill* and takes this author back to a time when he was a boy, the Cold War was still on and Sussex was being explored from the back of a 1982 Vauxhall Cavalier. To me still, the railway tunnel entrance at Amberley, although covered by a grill, is still Max Zorin's mine from where he hopes to blow up Silicon Valley and where Roger Moore and Grace Jones enter to stop Zorin and escape just in time; America's technical heartland being saved and the world a safer place once more. The late, great Sir Roger Moore may be alive no longer, but you can still see one of the locations where he played Bond for that one last time. It may have been perhaps years after he should have hung up his Walther PPK, but to me, it is Bond's greatest moment—and so West Sussex was where Bond *really* saved the world again. And talking of knowing when to finish, it is time that I wish you many happy hours exploring this half of the one-time kingdom of the South Saxons and hope you will join me in East Sussex in due course.

Further Reading and Information

For 'Visitors' Historic Sussex' talks and walking or motorized tours, please call All-Inclusive History on 07504 863867 or email info@ allinclusivehistory.org. Each one of these chapters can comprise an individual motorized tour, or on offer is a day or weekend tour of the whole county. Other tours are available including 'Lost Brighton', 'Royal Brighton', 'Business Brighton' and '*Brighton and Hove In 50 Buildings*'. All-Inclusive History also run a range of Sussex and Brighton-based events for businesses, organizations and schools.

Sussex Picnic Packs can be ordered to ensure you can be fed and watered as you explore Sussex. For a selection of bread, meat, salad, fruit, soft drinks and cheeses please contact Village Larder on hollie@villagelarder. co.uk or see www.villagelarder.co.uk. Picnic packs can be ordered and collected from Village Larder, Squires Garden Centre, Washington (near the centre of West Sussex) or call 01903 891744.

A Selection of Websites for Some Sites Mentioned (From West to East across West Sussex)

The Vandalian Tower: https://rosemaryandporkbelly.co.uk/vandalian-tower/

Chichester Harbour: http://peninsulapartnership.org.uk/abd/wp-content/ uploads/2012/12/Maritime-History-of-Chichester-Harbour.pdf

Harrow Hill: http://www.angmeringvillage.co.uk/history/harrowhill.htm

http://www.pastscape.org.uk/hob.aspx?hob_id=393091

Iping: http://roman-britain.co.uk/places/iping.htm

The Trundle: http://www.sussexarch.org.uk/saaf/trundle.html

Middleton Aircraft Works: http://www2.westsussex.gov.uk/learning-resources/ LR/norman_thompson_factory21fb.pdf?docid=d1c32f8b-05e1-4749-a33e-f1241bf7267c&version=-1

The Lost Village of Barpham: http://www.geograph.org.uk/photo/3583393

Park Brow: http://steyningmuseum.org.uk/parkbrow2.htm

http://www.westsussex.info/south-downs-way-wiston.shtml

Black Patch: http://www.findonvillage.com/0849_blackpatch_and_its_secrets.htm

Highdown: http://www.sussexarch.org.uk/saaf/highdown.html

Cissbury: http://www.westsussex.info/cissbury-ring.shtml; http://sussexarch.org.uk/saaf/cissbury.html

Round Hill, Steyning: http://www.steyningmuseum.org.uk/roundhill.htm

https://historicengland.org.uk/listing/the-list/list-entry/1005852

Steyning: http://www.hiddenbritainse.org.uk/test/steyning/towntrail_inside.pdf

Old Knepp Castle: http://www.knepp.co.uk/

Lost Knepp Village: http://www.knepp.co.uk/pages/history/New%20Articles/Possible%20DMV%20on%20Knepp%20estate.pdf

Gatwick Aviation Museum: http://www.gatwick-aviation-museum.co.uk/

Mouse Lane (Site of the 'Steyning To The Ring' memorial) http://steyningmuseum.org.uk/purvis3.htm

St Nicholas's Church, Old Shoreham: http://www.saintnicolas.org.uk/timeline.htm- The best website I've seen for any church in Sussex!

Devil's Dyke: http://www.pastscape.org.uk/hob.aspx?hob_id=399072

https://www.nationaltrust.org.uk/saddlescombe-farm-and-newtimber-hill/features/history-devils-dyke-ancient-footfalls-and-fortification

Ditchling Beacon: http://sussexarch.org.uk/saaf/ditchling.html; https://historicengland.org.uk/listing/the-list/list-entry/1015340

Worth Church: http://saxon.sussexchurches.co.uk/worth_1856.htm

Wolstonbury Hill: http://www.pastscape.org.uk/hob.aspx?hob_id=399066

A Select Bibliography

Argus/ Evening Argus Archives.

Armstrong, J.R., *A History of Sussex* (Phillimore, 1978).

Arscott, David, *Curiosities of West Sussex* (SR Publications, 1993).

Barr-Hamilton, Alex, *In Saxon Sussex* (Arundel Press, 1953).

Brandon, Peter and Short, Brian, *The South East From* AD *1000* (Longman, 1990).

Bryson, Bill, *At Home* (Doubleday, 2010).

Bunt, Peggy, *Viewing Sussex Series - Sussex Long Ago* (Warne, 1976).

Edmonds, Antony, *Lost Buildings of Worthing - A Historic Town and Its People* (Amberley, 2017).

Fraser, Antonia, *King Charles II (Part One)* (Orion, 2002 edition).

Gray, James S., *Victorian & Edwardian Sussex From Old Photographs* (Batsford, 1973).

Guy, John, *Castles of Sussex* (Philimore, 1984).

Harrison, David, *Along The South Downs* (Cassell, 1958).

Hayes, Martin and White, Emma (eds), *Great War Britain: West Sussex – Remembering 1914–18* (History Press, 2014).

Jamieson, Susan and Gina, *Old-Fashioned Days Out In Sussex* (Snake River Press, 2009).

Lang, Sean, *British History For Dummies* (Wiley, 2011).

Long, David, *Bizarre England* (O'Mara, 2015).

Longstaff-Tyrrell, Peter, *Front-Line Sussex: Napoleon Bonaparte To The Cold War* (Sutton, 2000).

Lucas, E.V., *Highways and Byways In Sussex* (1903).

Mais, S.P.B., *Sussex* (Richards Null, 1937).

Manley, John, *Atlas of Prehistoric Britain* (Phaidon, 1989).

Nairn, Ian and Pevsner, Nikolaus, *The Buildings of England - Sussex* (Puffin, 1965).

Newman, Kevin, *50 Gems of Sussex* (Amberley, 2017).

Newman, Kevin, *Brighton and Hove In 50 Buildings* (Amberley, 2016).

Newman, Kevin, *Brilliant Brighton* (The Argus, 2016).

Newman, Kevin, *Secret Brighton* (Amberley, 2016).

Newman, Kevin, *Super Sussex* (The Argus, 2017).

Ollard, Richard, *The Escape of Charles II* (Robinson, 2002).

Parsons, David and Milner-Gulland, Robin, *Churches and Chapels of The South Downs National Park* (Sussexpast, 2017).

Pennington, Janet, 'Chanctonbury Ring - The Story of A Sussex Landmark', (Downland History Publishing, 2011).

Sauvain, Philip, *Imagining The Past: Prehistoric Britain* (Macmillan, 1978).

Sussex Archaeological Collections - Volumes 139 & 140 (Sussex Archaeological Society, 2000 & 2001).

Thomas-Stanford, Charles, *Sussex In The Great Civil War* (Chiswick, 1910).

Venning, Timothy, *The Kings & Queens of Anglo-Saxon England* (Amberley, 2013).

Victoria County History 'Sussex' – various.

Waugh, Mary, *Smuggling in Kent & Sussex 1700–1840* (Countryside Books, 1985).

Index